OTHER BOOKS BY PENELOPE CASAS

The Foods and Wines of Spain

Tapas: The Little Dishes of Spain

Discovering Spain: An Uncommon Guide

¡Delicioso! The Regional Cooking of Spain

PAELLA!

PAELLA!

Spectacular Rice Dishes from Spain

Penelope Casas

HENRY HOLT AND COMPANY ～ NEW YORK

Henry Holt and Company, LLC
Publishers since 1866
175 Fifth Avenue
New York, New York 10010
www.henryholt.com

Henry Holt® and *® are registered trademarks*
of Henry Holt and Company, LLC.

Library of Congress Cataloging-in-Publication Data
Casas, Penelope.
Paella!: spectacular rice dishes from Spain / Penelope Casas.
p.   cm.
Includes index.
ISBN-13: 978-0-8050-5623-5
ISBN-10: 0-8050-5623-8
1. Cookery (Rice)   I. Title.
TX809.R5C36   1999
641.8'2—dc21   98-34727

Henry Holt books are available for special
promotions and premiums. For details contact:
Director, Special Markets.

First Edition 1999

Designed by Paula Russell Szafranski
Photographs by Luis Casas
Frontispiece: La Pepica, Valencia

Printed in the United States of America

13   15   17   19   20   18   16   14

To Luis—

My paella partner for the past thirty years

Contents

Acknowledgments   ix

A Passion for Paella   3

Seafood Paellas   15

Meat, Poultry, and Game Paellas   67

Mixed Meat and Seafood Paellas   119

Vegetable Paellas   129

Tapas and First Courses   151

Desserts   181

Broths, Sauces, and Dips   205

Sources for Spanish Products   215

Index   217

Acknowledgments

Although the eminently agreeable task of preparing more than sixty different paellas in my home kitchen fell to me alone, the search for the secrets of rice cookery in Spain and my quest for the finest paellas led me, as always, to Spanish friends, both new and old, to many fine restaurants in Spain that I have come to love and admire over the years, and to others I discovered while investigating paella.

Through their creativity, boundless energy, and enthusiasm, my friends Reme and Ximo Boix of Tasca del Puerto restaurant introduced me over the years to wonderful rice dishes from their native Castellón de la Plana. And I am not likely to ever forget the paella bash that Ximo and his teenage son Nacho (a budding chef) cooked up over an open fire for five hundred bikers in an isolated mountain setting not far from the Mediterranean coast.

Pepe Piera of El Pegolí in Denia, despite his sometimes forbidding demeanor, has always been the soul of generosity, heaping kilo upon kilo of rare Valencian *bomba* rice on me to enrich my paellas in New York. His wife and his daughter, Mariluz, took me into their pint-size kitchen and divulged the secrets of their magnificent Arroz a Banda, a dish that has been a passion of mine for over twenty years.

Gonzalo Córdoba, restaurateur *por excelencia*, never fails to prepare a lunch based on paella every time my husband and I visit his restaurant El

Faro in Cádiz, our favorite Spanish city. Although Cádiz is far from paella's homeland, at El Faro the rice is always outstanding, and Gonzalo never hesitates to share his recipes with me.

Juanjo at Casa Roberto in Valencia is a more recent acquaintance but equally forthcoming. He invited me into his kitchen to observe every step involved in his prize-winning lobster paella and shared some tricks of the trade with me. At La Pepica, also in Valencia, paella reigns supreme, and Doña Juanita, the grande dame of paella, still holds court at ninety years of age. She greets us at the door, regales us with stories of the good old days, and bestows upon us her considerable knowledge and experience.

Thanks also to all the fine restaurants in the Levante that keep local culinary traditions alive, and especially to those that make our visits to the region so memorable: Racó d'Olla in El Palmar; La Dársena in Alicante; Casa del Mar in Lo Pagán, Murcia; Galbis in L'Alcudia; and Casa Salvador in Cullera. All the chefs at these restaurants are truly paella maestros.

I thank my daughter, Elisa, who planted the idea in my mind for a paella cookbook and persuaded me to follow through; her husband, Steve, whose business savvy was invaluable in helping me navigate my way through the ins and outs of international publishing, and my parents, Toni and Chick, who were always at hand to offer advice and support. Marsha Stanton, the finest friend anyone could hope for, although hardly a cook herself, contributed her near clairvoyant sense of what tastes good and which seemingly unlikely ingredients would marry exceptionally well. She became my sounding board for new paella recipes, and by bouncing ideas off her I was able to make some good paellas into extraordinary ones. When my husband and I were no longer capable of finishing the paellas that continued to emerge from my kitchen, we dropped them off with her doorman. She eagerly accepted and ate with gusto each and every one and offered her perceptive critique.

My husband, Luis, has always been an integral part of my writing career, offering staunch support and encouragement. He is my most reliable critic, editor, constant travel companion. We have crisscrossed Spain for decades, sharing wonderful experiences and endless good times.

Tino Salcedo, representative in New York for IVEX—an organization dedicated to advancing Valencian products—arranged the fascinating excursion I took through the rice fields of Valencia and provided me with Valencian food supplies, while Zaida Rivera Alcalde of Med Foods in Alexandria, Virginia, unhesitantly replenished my continually dwindling supplies of rice, saffron, and olive oil.

My deepest appreciation to Ignacio Vasallo for his assistance and good cheer, to my good friend and colleague, Pilar Vico, for her unstinting support of all my projects, and to José Carlos Fernández for his swift and efficient attention to all my travel needs. Janet Kafka, ardent promotor of all things Spanish, was, as always, exceptionally generous with her time and expertise.

For every one of my books I owe a deep debt of gratitude to my friend and mentor, Craig Claiborne, who launched my writing career and has remained a good friend. And I thank my editor, Beth Crossman, for her enthusiastic support of this project and her unswerving belief in its success.

PAELLA!

A Passion for Paella

Valencia: Home of Paella

Clearing Up a Few Misconceptions

Tips for a Perfect Paella

A Few Tricks

Pairing Spanish Wines with Paella

Paella, among the best known and most beloved dishes in the world, has been my passion ever since I first tasted it in Spain over thirty years ago. And yet I have little enthusiasm for the paellas I have eaten outside of Spain. The horrors that have befallen this exquisite dish and the indignities it has suffered!

Paella transforms rice, the sustenance of at least half of the world's population, into a brilliantly complex and exceedingly baroque creation. Praise for paella comes from all quarters, and paella recipes appear in most all-purpose American cookbooks. Yet even the most respected chefs and cookbook authors have little understanding of how extraordinary paella can be when authentically prepared. They have perpetuated misconceptions that continue to deprive Americans who eat out and cook at home of the true greatness of paella.

Paella is not a steamed rice, cooked in a covered pan, but generally a "dry" rice that cooks uncovered in a wide, flat paella pan. It is not bright orange (that comes from artificial coloring), and it is not a precooked pot of Uncle Ben's rice to which lobster, chicken, and clams have been strewn on top to give a pretty appearance and to disguise what is usually very ordinary rice. Garnishes, in fact, are totally secondary to paella and among their least important features. A paella should never be judged by its toppings; paella is visually striking in itself and needs little additional adornment. The texture and flavor of the rice is everything, and that flavor depends on the ingredients that are combined with the rice and from which the rice soaks up its flavors. Plain rice, after all, is like a painter's canvas waiting to be transformed into a work of art.

For me, the best paella is not the typical mixture of seafood, meat, and sausage that we have come to call paella. Such paellas are frowned upon in Valencia, the area of Spain that is paella's homeland, because they do not allow each ingredient to be savored and appreciated on its own merits. The best paellas highlight special ingredients—meat, fish, or vegetables. That is why you will find only a handful of so-called mixed paellas in this book.

Authentic paella is always made with short-grain rice because it absorbs flavors far more readily than long-grain converted rice (which is parboiled before you buy it) and is immensely more exciting in taste and texture. Serious cooks would not dream of using long-grain rice to make risotto, so why accept it in paella where it is equally inappropriate? The cooking methods and ingredients for paella and risotto may not be the same, but the concept of combining short-grain rice with a variety of ingredients is indeed quite similar.

My mission is to rescue the glorious paella that I know and love from worldwide ignominy, where it has languished for decades. The time is ripe; interest in grains and in the health-giving Mediterranean diet is at an all-time high. And the Spanish diet in particular, based on the robust flavors of olive oil, garlic, tomatoes, and peppers—all of which enter into paella—has put Spain in the enviable position as the country with the world's third highest life expectancy. Paella represents just one region of Spain, and each region is a world unto itself. Indeed, Spain compresses the variety of a continent into a country no bigger than Texas. You will find regions of soaring peaks, vast plains, deserts, and thick forests—each with its distinctive culture, a product of many ancient civilizations that passed through the Iberian Peninsula and left their mark.

Cooking in Spain is equally varied: extraordinary seafood along the extensive coast; baby lamb and suckling pig, roasted in brick vaulted ovens from the plains of Castile; gazpacho and cooling vinaigrettes from the south, where a strong Moorish influence brought the scents of cumin, coriander, and nutmeg to the cooking; and, of course, paella from the eastern coast, often called the Region of the Rices.

Correcting preconceived notions about paella has certainly been an uphill battle, but progress has been made. Some restaurants in America are now preparing paellas in the traditional manner, and my hope is that *Paella!* will make Americans realize what they have been missing all these years. Curiously, despite its mistreatment, paella's popularity never fades, no matter what the food fashion of the moment happens to be.

Valencia: Home of Paella

A trip to Spain for me is never complete without a visit to paella's native land, the region on Spain's eastern coast officially designated País Valencià (Valencian Country), but commonly called El Levante (land of the rising sun, because it is here that Spain greets the day). El Levante also refers to Murcia, the region to the south that also produces and prepares rice. The País Valencià comprises the provinces of Castellón de la Plana, Valencia, and Alicante, and as you head south close to the Mediterranean coast, you will discover the region's special beauty: In the narrow corridor between the rugged imposing mountains to the west and the sea, the mighty rivers Júcar and Turia deposit rich alluvial soil, forming pancake-flat land. In this warm, humid, sun-drenched area, everything thrives, creating what is often called the Garden of Spain. Orange trees beyond number carpet the land in the province of Castellón de la Plana; farther south as you approach Valencia, small family plots (*huertas*), which produce the glistening fresh vegetables that are important to every paella, begin to appear. Once past the city of Valencia, vast rice fields dominate the landscape, creating a veritable carpet of bright green rice shoots in summer that competes in beauty with the nearby deep blue Mediterranean.

In the rice fields, stooped laborers shaded from the sun by wide-brimmed straw hats plod the marshy land, and whitewashed, straw-thatched workers' cottages (*barracas*) dot the rice paddies. The immense lagoon of La Albufera ("little sea" in the Arab tongue) forms the nexus between the swampy rice fields and the Mediterranean; crude, single-sailed sampanlike boats ply the water that is alive with eels, jumping fish, croaking frogs, and aquatic birds. Few sights in Spain rival the splendor and tranquility of a sunset over La Albufera. The Albufera and the rice fields always cast a spell on me; it's as if I have left Spain and entered some magical, exotic land.

The bounty of El Levante, showcased at Valencia's enormous central market, would not have been possible without the ingenuity of the Moors, who arrived from North Africa almost thirteen hundred years ago. They created elaborate irrigation systems to channel river water from the mountains that otherwise would be lost to the sea. To this day a water tribunal composed of town elders meets every Thursday morning on the steps of Valencia's cathedral to settle water disputes, and although they are not backed by any legal authority, their decisions are ironclad; there is no higher court of appeal. The Moors also introduced rice, known by its Moorish name, *arroz*, to the region, as well as saffron (an Arab word that refers to the yellow color saffron gives). All this set the scene for the creation of paella several centuries later. Many paellas are in fact called *arroz con* (rice with) followed by the names of the key ingredients.

Paella bestows an aura on the Valencia region, for it is not merely a regional food specialty but part of the very fiber of Valencian life. It is a diet staple, eaten daily, usually for lunch, the main meal of the day, and occasionally for dinner (Valencians consume more than fifty pounds of rice per person each year). Depending on what is combined with the rice, paella can be a poor man's meal or a deluxe extravaganza.

Paella in Valencia simply cannot be surpassed. Although the region's water is not among the tastiest to drink (and just try to rinse the suds from your hair with it), when it is used to cook the rice (or to make broth for the rice), it contributes to a perfect paella. Then there is the rice itself, local varieties that are short grained and low in starch. Particularly outstanding is *arroz bomba*, a relatively rare rice used by some of the best restaurants, which expands like an accordion when cooked and is unique in texture (to obtain it, see Sources, page 215).

The region's long tradition of preparing rice has made every Valencian a master of paella. Men who wouldn't dream of entering the kitchen are often in charge of an outdoor paella. There are also authentic paella maestros, known in the region for their superlative skills. These chefs often take their shows on the road, organizing paella fests for hundreds (even thousands), and the entire meal is made in a single paella pan. The *Guinness Book of World Records* lists a paella for fifty thousand people made with ten thousand pounds of rice in a paella pan sixty feet across. Although I did not witness that event, I was present for a paella made for five hundred by my friend Ximo and his son Nacho from La Tasca del Puerto restaurant. Organized in a remote setting in the mountains west of Castellón de la Plana, it was a lively outdoor summer affair. As impossible as it may seem, the paella was cooked to perfection.

So many of my fondest remembrances of Spain are connected to paella, and I am still sometimes surprised at the lengths to which my husband, Luis, and I will go to eat our favorite paellas. We once drove like demons to reach La Tasca del Puerto, portside in Castellón de la Plana, before dining hours were over because we craved the restaurant's sensational Black Squid Rice. On another occasion we braved a torrential downpour that threatened to engulf our car because we didn't want to miss tasting a few of the fifty different paellas on the menu each day at La Dársena in Alicante. We sat impatiently in a colossal traffic jam between Valencia and Denia, never considering turning back, for the exquisite pleasure of eating El Pegolí's one and only paella, Arroz a Banda. When we travel to Valencia, we never pass up eating a paella outdoors at Racó d'Olla while the sun sets over the Albufera lagoon. And we always take a ride to the city's beach near the port to pay our respects to ninety-year-old Juanita, owner of the venerable La Pepica restaurant, paella mecca of the world and once a favorite of Ernest Hemingway. There we look forward to a paella made the old-fashioned way—over a wood-burning stove and brought to the table for our approval before serving. Later a dish of *socarrat*—crisp rice scraped from the bottom of the pan, the crowning jewel of a well-made paella—is presented to us with great pride and ceremony.

Although *Paella!* includes all the traditional paellas I have enjoyed for years in Spain, there are many unconventional ones here as well that do not appear on menus in Spain, in Spanish cookbooks, or at Spanish tables. The revolution in cooking that took Spain by storm in the seventies did not bring change to paella, and I also had limited myself to a handful of tried-and-true paella recipes. For this book, however, I experimented with new combinations, always based on Spanish ingredients and sometimes on traditional dishes that do not normally include rice. It was a venture that produced some sensational new paellas and I think takes paella to a new dimension. My hope is that you too will find pleasure in exploring paella's endless possibilities. *¡Buen provecho!*

Clearing Up a Few Misconceptions

Isn't paella just one dish? Since I announced my intention to write an entire cookbook on the subject of paella, I have been asked this question time and time again. Paella is most certainly not one dish; it is endless dishes made with almost any ingredient. It is a technique for making many rice dishes that are generally united by the eye-catching paella pan (the word *paella* comes from the Latin word *patella*, meaning pan) in which they cook and by their cooking method. The only indispensable ingredients are rice, water, and olive oil. Everything else is the subject of endless debates and discussions by Spaniards, who love a lively discussion and consider their own recipe the one and only. Paellas are as free-spirited as the cooks who prepare them; once the technique is mastered, the sky is the limit. Indeed, after completing *Paella!* I realized that I had just begun exploring paella's diversity.

Isn't paella difficult to make? Not at all, and although it makes a splendid party dish (for which most of the preparation can be done in advance), it is just as appropriate for quiet nights at home.

Isn't making paella time-consuming? Paella takes no more time to make than any other meal made from fresh, healthy ingredients. Keep in mind that the entire meal is in the paella pan; there is no need to prepare side courses, and cleanup is minimal. To further simplify a meal based on paella, *Paella!* includes both appetizers and desserts that are easy, quick, and ideal accompaniments to paella. You can focus your attention on the paella and still have a splendid three-course meal.

Doesn't paella require special equipment and ingredients? While the time-honored paella pan is best for making most paellas, shallow casseroles also work well. It is certainly not necessary to invest in an expensive stainless-steel paella pan. Paella chefs, in fact, are disdainful of them and prefer the traditional thin-metal, wide-bottomed, shallow pans that heat like lightning and immediately adjust to changes in temperature.

Most ingredients in a paella are common supermarket items. Even when a few more unusual ingredients are suggested, I have made every effort to offer everyday substitutes.

Tips for a Perfect Paella

❧ Recipes may be halved or doubled without any change in ingredient proportions.

❧ Have all ingredients chopped and measured before beginning the final cooking of the paella; it is a quick-cooking dish that, not unlike dishes in Chinese cooking, must have all ingredients ready to go. This can be done well in advance, especially when cooking for guests. To cut down on time, have your butcher or fishmonger cut up your meats and fish. Some frozen vegetables, as indicated in the recipes, work as well or better than fresh.

❧ Since clams and mussels, when called for, are generally cooked directly in the rice, they must first be purged of grit by soaking them in water. Scrub the mussels or clams and rinse well, then place in a bowl of salted water to cover. Sprinkle with about 1 tablespoon cornmeal, bread crumbs, or flour and refrigerate several hours or overnight. Rinse well before using.

❧ Sprinkle other seafood with kosher or sea salt about ten minutes before cooking to help bring back the briny taste of the sea that most seafood, especially frozen seafood, tends to lose.

❧ Keep the measured broth very hot but not boiling, before beginning the final cooking. If it boils, some will evaporate, and you will be short of liquid. The success of a paella is directly related to the depth of flavor of its broth. Canned chicken and vegetable broths and bottled clam juice are perfectly acceptable, but, if possible, enhance them as described on page 207 with herbs, onions, and other flavor boosters. Best of all, make your own broths from the recipes in Chapter 8.

❧ Ingredients such as nuts, garlic, and parsley are often mashed to a paste in a ceramic or stone mortar or in a miniprocessor to release their full flavor. The mortar (one of civilization's ancient cooking tools) does a better job and is simpler to use and to clean than a miniprocessor. I would never be without a mortar in the kitchen. Try it.

❧ A paella pan is specifically designed to cook paella. Wide, very flat, and with low sides sloping outward, the authentic cheap metal pans (not heavy stainless steel; see Sources, page 215) are still the best to cook the rice so that it is low in moisture and al dente. Even with the best of care these pans will darken and discolor with use, and will rust if left wet. Therefore, after making a paella, rinse with water and remove any scraps with a stiff brush, clean with steel wool soap pads (the pan cleans quite easily), rinse, and dry immediately and thoroughly with paper towels. Let the pan sit a few minutes to continue drying, then apply a light coating of olive oil with a paper towel before storing. You can, however, make a good paella in a stainless-steel paella pan or in any wide, flat-bottomed casserole dish that can go from burner to oven.

❧ Sauté your "aromatics" (onion, garlic, peppers, tomato, and so forth) in olive oil as indicated in each recipe. Paprika is an especially important addition to most paellas; do make an effort to buy Spanish smoked paprika, which gives an extraordinary flavor to paella (see Sources, page 215). Another typically Spanish ingredient requisite in several paella recipes are *ñoras*, dried sweet red peppers (much more common in Spain's cooking than chile peppers); they give a golden color to the rice and lend their distinctive flavor.

 ❧ Once the rice is added, stir to coat well with the pan mixture so that the rice absorbs the olive oil and is thus sealed, preventing the rice from releasing its starch and keeping it firm.

 ❧ Short-grain rice imported from Spain (see Sources, page 215) gives the most authentic results: firm, dry, and al dente. Unique *bomba* rice from Valencia is incomparable (but note that this rice requires a little more liquid—about ⅓ cup more for 3 cups of rice—and may take a few extra minutes to cook). Italian Arborio, although yielding a creamier rice, is more than acceptable. (The Italian rice that I find works particularly well is Beretta Superfino Arborio.)

 ❧ Olive oil is essential to a paella. Make sure it is a good one, but you should not use your best extra-virgin oil (save that for the sauces and dips and for some of the first-course recipes). While you are exploring Spanish paellas, why not also get acquainted with the splendid olive oils from Spain? Their flavor is distinctive, and I consider them the world's finest.

 ❧ Although all recipes call for saffron, which is either softened in the broth or mashed with other ingredients in a mortar or miniprocessor, it is not essential. I have eaten great paellas even in Valencia that omitted saffron. But if you use saffron, make sure it is genuine, pure saffron from Spain, and buy it from a reputable source. Buy it in threads (not ground) to better judge its color and quality. Saffron is very expensive, but a very small amount goes a long way. If it is stored in a tin or covered glass jar away from light, it will last indefinitely.

 ❧ When you add the hot cooking liquid to the rice, bring it to a boil, stirring occasionally, and continue to boil until the rice is no longer soupy but sufficient liquid remains to continue cooking the rice. This takes about 5 minutes, and when this point has been reached, the bubbles rising from the pan will look slightly thick, most of the rice will appear at the surface, and a spoon will momentarily leave a path exposing the bottom of the pan when pulled through the center of the rice.

 ❧ Electric ovens, even when properly calibrated, seem to cook paella more slowly than gas ovens. For electric ovens, raise the temperature by 50° and increase the cooking time by 5–8 minutes. Transfer the paella to the oven, uncovered, for final cooking. At this stage the rice should never be disturbed by stirring. Although paella may also be completed on top of the stove, the burners are usually not wide enough to provide even heat to all parts of the paella pan. Finishing the paella in the oven is the most foolproof method.

 ❧ Never cook paella until the rice is completely done. If you do, it will be mushy by the time it reaches the table. Remove from the oven when the rice grains are no longer hard but still have more bite than you want and a crust forms around the edge of the pan. Paella must rest five to ten minutes after being removed from the oven, during which time the final cooking takes place.

 ❧ Paella can be prepared in advance, up to and including the addition of the rice, and kept at room temperature for several hours before completion.

❧ Some paella recipes call for specific garnishes, but if not, leave the paella as is or garnish with pimiento strips and/or minced parsley. Both are always suitable and give some added color.

❧ *Socarrat,* the crisp rice that sticks to the bottom of the pan, is considered a delicacy. But if paella is not made over a wood-burning fire, you are not likely to achieve a *socarrat*. Simulate it by placing the completed paella over very high heat until it begins to stick to the pan and turn crisp. Some recipes give instructions for making *socarrat*, but a *socarrat* is appropriate with any paella.

❧ Always bring the paella to the table in its pan for diners to admire before serving. Traditionally, paella is eaten communally: Everyone sits around the pan and takes the rice directly from the pan with a spoon. Although you are not likely to serve it this way, do leave the paella pan at the center of the table so guests can help themselves to more.

A Few Tricks

❧ If your paella is almost al dente and ready to be removed from the oven but still seems to have liquid, return it to the top of the stove over high heat, without stirring, until the liquid has evaporated. Then proceed to cover the rice and let it rest.

❧ If the paella is dry before the rice is almost al dente, sprinkle with a few tablespoons of water and allow to cook in the oven 2–3 minutes longer.

❧ Paella is still delicious the next day, although never quite the same as freshly made paella. To keep leftovers, remove the paella from the paella pan (otherwise a slightly metallic taste may develop) and store in the refrigerator (not in the freezer because freezing changes the consistency of the rice). Paella reheats best in the microwave.

❧ Paella cooked over wood or charcoal will attain a subtle smoky flavor, a result of the smoke that circulates around and over the paella pan. An outdoor paella is a little difficult to do because the heat must be strong but not so strong that it burns the rice. Place the paella pan on a grill about 16 inches from the flame. Sauté your ingredients in the paella pan, just as you would on the stove, then cook the rice as directed in any paella recipe. Instead of placing it in the oven, remove from the flame when almost al dente and let sit a few minutes in a warm spot to finish cooking. For better heat control, use a gas barbecue. Better still, purchase a gas ring grill specifically designed for paellas (see Sources, page 215).

Pairing Spanish Wines with Paella

Wines from Spain are readily available in America, and they are world class. While appropriate with foods of any nation, they are particularly suited to Spanish foods since both spring from the same earth and seem to have a natural affinity for each other.

Although many paellas are based on seafood, red wines are nonetheless generally more appropriate because of the complex and assertive flavors found in paella. For delicately flavored paellas, however, such as Scallop and Mushroom Paella, I highly recommend an elegant dry Albariño white wine, such as Martín Códax or Condes de Albarei from the northwest region of Galicia. For relatively light seafood paellas try the outstanding white wines from Rueda in Castile, like Marqués de Riscal, or a Catalan white such as Juvé y Camps Ermita D'Espiells. For more strongly flavored seafood paellas—Black Squid Paella, for example—nothing could be better than a light-bodied Rioja red wine; Viña Cumbrero and Remelluri are two great choices.

Poultry, rabbit, game, pork, and lamb paellas also stand up well to red Riojas and to the crisp, highly praised Ribera del Duero reds that are capturing international attention. Try Yllera, Protos, and Pesquera.

Sangria, the original wine cooler, a mix of red or white wine with sugar, citric juices, and sparkling water, is a great drink to accompany a beachside paella. Otherwise, Spaniards much prefer to pair paella with a good wine.

Spanish sherries—dry sherries as aperitifs, sweet sherries as dessert wines—are discussed in the Tapas and First Courses chapter and in Desserts, respectively.

Seafood Paellas

Scallop and Mushroom Paella

Scallop, Shrimp, and Seaweed Paella

Shrimp Paella with Salmorreta Red Pepper Sauce

Rosemary-Scented Shellfish and Egg Paella

Golden Rice with Shrimp and Fresh Tuna

Pesto Shellfish Paella

Soupy Rice with Shellfish

Garlicky Clam Paella

Mussel Paella

Lobster Paella "Casa Roberto"

Crabmeat Paella with Peas

Stewed Squid Paella "El Faro"

Black Squid Paella

Squid and Scallion Paella

Mixed Seafood Paella

"Rice on Its Own" El Pegolí

Seafood Rice, Murcia Style

Seafood Pasta Paella

Monkfish, Swiss Chard, and Sesame Seed Paella

Monkfish and Almond Paella, Alicante Style

Salmon and Asparagus Paella with Capers and Dill

Cod, Beans, and Hot Green Pepper Paella

Cod, Cauliflower, and Artichoke Paella

Cod Paella, Catalan Style

RICE: THE LIFE-GIVING GRAIN

A staple of Eastern civilizations for over five thousand years, rice is esteemed for its low calories, absence of fat, and high content of minerals and carbohydrates. It eventually reached Europe when Arab invasions brought the culture and cooking of the Orient to the West. In southeastern Spain, where Moorish influence remained strong for almost eight hundred years, rice became an important part of the local diet. Warm temperatures, bright sunshine, relatively high humidity, and an abundance of water created ideal conditions for growing rice in Valencia and Murcia, in southern Catalunya and in western Andalucía. Rice traveled to the New World by way of Spanish conquerors and colonizers, where it was also integrated into the native diet.

Growing rice is a labor intensive process. It begins by channeling the water supply that flows from the mountains and regulating the amount of water coming into and out of the fields. The Moors accomplished these tasks hundreds of years ago, and their ingenious system of canals (*acequias*) is still in use today.

In the Valencia region, seeds are sown from April to early May in very shallow water. As the rice plants grow, the water supply is gradually increased, until it reaches a depth of about six inches. Weeding occupies the summer months, and from mid-September to October the rice plants—now dry and yellowed after intentionally being deprived of water—are harvested. They are left to dry completely—traditionally in the sun—before the grain is separated from the chaff, in a process similar to threshing wheat. The dark outer layer of the rice is left intact for brown rice and polished off for white rice.

Spaniards prefer short-grain rices, although in western Andalucía long grain is grown, principally for export to the United States. Calasparra rice, the only Spanish rice with its own denomination of origin, is an excellent product that is grown in the mountains of Murcia. Renowned *bomba* rice (see Sources, page 215), another short-grain rice with a unique texture that resists overcooking, had practically disappeared from Spain because of its high production costs. A fragile grain, *arroz bomba* needs extra special care and is prone to weather-related damage. But as Spain awakened to the Gourmet Age, interest in such fine products by both restaurants and consumers saved *bomba* rice from extinction. Today rice growers devote more and more acreage to *arroz bomba* to cope with an ever-growing demand. It is more expensive than other rices, but well worth using for the subtle and elusive difference it brings to paella.

Scallop and Mushroom Paella

(Arroz con Vieiras y Setas)

While most paellas tend to have lively, forceful flavors, this one is wonderfully delicate. It is not a traditional preparation (scallops are found in Spain only along the northwestern coast of Galicia, not in the Valencia region). This recipe was inspired by a dish created by Toñi Vicente, a talented chef at a restaurant of the same name in the historic city of Santiago de Compostela.

Serves 6

1 pound bay scallops or sea scallops cut in half	5 tablespoons olive oil
Kosher or sea salt	6 tablespoons minced shallots
4½ cups clam juice or Fish Broth (page 208)	½ pound oyster or other mild-flavored mushrooms, brushed clean, thick stems trimmed, and coarsely chopped
½ cup dry white wine	
2 tablespoons freshly squeezed lemon juice	4 tablespoons minced parsley
¼ teaspoon crumbled thread saffron	¼ cup diced Spanish serrano ham or prosciutto, cut from a ¼-inch-thick slice
2 teaspoons fresh thyme leaves or ¼ teaspoon dried	2½ cups imported Spanish or Arborio short-grain rice
2 teaspoons chopped fresh rosemary leaves or ¼ teaspoon dried	Lemon wedges for garnish

Sprinkle the scallops all over with salt and let sit at room temperature.

Combine the clam juice with the wine, lemon juice, saffron, thyme, and rosemary. Keep hot over the lowest heat.

Preheat the oven to 400° F for gas oven, 450° F for electric.

Heat the oil in a paella pan measuring 17–18 inches at its widest point (or in a shallow casserole of a similar size), over 2 burners if necessary. Sauté the scallops over high heat for about 1 minute, then remove to a warm platter (they should not be fully cooked).

Lower the heat, add the shallots, and cook 1 minute. Stir in the mushrooms, 2 tablespoons of the parsley, and the ham, and sauté 2 minutes more. Add the rice and stir to coat well with the pan mixture.

Pour in all the hot broth and bring to a boil. Taste for salt and continue boiling for about 5 minutes, stirring and rotating the pan occasionally, until the rice is no longer soupy but sufficient liquid remains to continue cooking the rice. Stir in the scallops and any juices from the platter and transfer to the oven. Cook, uncovered, until the rice is almost al dente, about 10–12 minutes in a gas oven, 15–20 minutes electric.

Remove to a warm spot, cover with foil, and let sit 5–10 minutes more. Sprinkle with the remaining 2 tablespoons parsley and garnish with lemon wedges.

Scallop, Shrimp, and Seaweed Paella

(Paella de Vieiras, Gambas, y Algas)

The assertive taste of seaweed in this unforgettable paella is the perfect complement to the delicate flavor of the shrimp and scallops. It is also among the simplest paellas to make. If you wish to garnish the paella, buy some extra-large shrimp (about two per person), sauté them with the other seafood, and arrange over the paella just before putting it in the oven. Dried seaweed is available in health food stores and Asian food markets.

Serves 6 to 8

1 pound bay scallops or sea
    scallops cut in half
1 pound shrimp, shelled and cut
    crosswise in ½-inch pieces
Kosher or sea salt
1 cup dried seaweed, such as Fueru
    Wakame
5½ cups bottled clam juice or Fish
    Broth (page 208)
¼ teaspoon crumbled thread
    saffron
½ cup dry white wine

2 tablespoons freshly squeezed
    lemon juice
6 tablespoons olive oil
2 medium green bell peppers,
    finely chopped
4 tablespoons finely chopped
    shallots
1⅓ cups well washed, finely
    chopped leeks, white part only
2 tablespoons minced parsley
3 cups imported Spanish or
    Arborio short-grain rice

Sprinkle the scallops and shrimp with salt and let sit 15 minutes. Soak the seaweed in warm water to cover until softened. Drain and dry between paper towels.

Combine the clam juice, saffron, wine, and lemon juice, and keep hot over the lowest heat. Preheat the oven to 400° F for gas oven, 450° F for electric.

Heat the oil in a paella pan measuring 17–18 inches at its widest point (or in a shallow casserole of a similar size), over 2 burners if necessary. Sauté the scallops and shrimp over high heat about 1 minute, turning once, until the seafood just turns opaque on the surface. Remove to a warm platter. Add the green peppers, and sauté until slightly softened. Stir in the shallots and leeks, and cook 1 minute, then add the seaweed, parsley, and rice, stirring to coat the rice well with the pan mixture. Pour in all the hot liquid and bring to a boil. Taste for salt and continue boiling, stirring and rotating the pan occasionally, until the rice is no longer soupy but sufficient liquid remains to continue cooking the rice, about 5 minutes. Stir in the reserved scallops and shrimp and any juices from the platter.

Transfer to the oven and cook, uncovered, about 10–12 minutes in a gas oven, 15–20 minutes electric, until the rice is almost al dente. Remove to a warm spot, cover with foil, and let sit 5–10 minutes, until the rice is cooked to taste.

OLIVE OIL:
SPAIN'S GOLDEN ELIXIR

It is no longer a secret that olive oil is good for you. Scientific studies have proved what Mediterraneans have intuitively known since time immemorial, and the data are most persuasive: olive oil is a mono-unsaturated fat that can naturally help lower cholesterol; it facilitates digestion, is high in many essential vitamins, and contributes to healthy hearts and sound arteries.

Spain is the world's largest producer of olive oil and has been so ever since the Romans brought olive trees to Spain. The climate is ideal, especially in Catalunya and in Andalucía; Andalucía alone yields a full 20 percent of world production. There, olive trees thrive, stretching in unending rows, up and down the dry hilly terrain, their silver leaves glimmering in the bright sunlight. Whereas Catalunya produces smooth, subtle oils, generally from the Arbequina olive, the oils of Andalucía tend to be wonderfully robust and fruity, products of the Picual and Picudo olives.

The cooking of Spain relies on olive oil, and it is an indispensable ingredient in all paellas. It also fries foods wonderfully well and is even used for certain desserts (two fine examples are the Peach Yogurt Torte and Oranges in Honey and Olive Oil "Nuñez de Prado" found in this book).

Olive oils labeled "pure" are those that are most appropriate for general cooking. The finest extra-virgin oils, on the other hand, lose their complexity and fine aroma if subjected to prolonged heating. Such exquisite oils should be reserved for dishes in which they will shine. I like to use them to marinate foods, to dress salads, to coat pastas, and to drizzle on bread.

Whether you choose mild or assertive olive oil is a matter of personal taste. For my basic cooking needs I use olive oils from Spain that I find in supermarkets and in Hispanic and Italian delicatessens, like Sabroso and Itálica. But when I want the very best I choose Nuñez de Prado, Mas Portell, or Rafael Salgado, available in food specialty shops or at The Spanish Table (see Sources, page 215).

Shrimp Paella with Salmorreta Red Pepper Sauce

(Arroz con Gambas y Salsa Salmorreta)

This is a glorious paella in the Alicante style in which the distinctive broth, made with dried red peppers (or paprika) and tomato, lends the characteristic Alicante flavor to the rice. If the broth and the delicious salmorreta sauce, also made with dried red peppers and tomatoes, and fortified with garlic and olive oil, are prepared in advance, the rest is a breeze. Although making the broth with fresh clams gives more concentrated flavor, clam juice may be substituted. The salmorreta sauce is served on the side and is equally good with the rice or as a dip for the large shrimp. It can be omitted, but if you take the extra time to make it, the paella will be noticeably enriched.

Serves 6 to 8

BROTH

8 cups water or clam juice

1 dozen large clams, cleansed
    (page 10)

¼ teaspoon crumbled thread
    saffron

Salt

2 sprigs parsley

1 pound small to medium shrimp
    in their shells

Salmorreta Red Pepper Sauce
    (page 209)

16 to 24 extra-large shrimp in their
    shells, preferably with heads

2 large cleaned squid (about
    ½ pound), with or without
    tentacles, finely chopped

2 dried sweet red peppers, (*ñoras*;
    see Sources, page 215) or mild
    New Mexico peppers, cored
    and seeded (otherwise use
    2 tablespoons sweet paprika,
    preferably Spanish smoked, and
    1 fresh red bell pepper)

4 small whole tomatoes

8 tablespoons olive oil

12 cloves garlic, minced

2 tablespoons minced parsley

1 teaspoon sweet paprika,
    preferably Spanish
    smoked

3 cups imported Spanish or
    Arborio short-grain rice

To make the broth, combine in a large pot the water, clams, saffron, salt, parsley, dried peppers, and tomatoes. Shell the small shrimp and add the shells to the broth. Bring to a boil and simmer about 30 minutes. Remove the dried peppers and 2 of the tomatoes to a platter. Strain the rest of the broth, pressing with the back of a wooden spoon to extract as much liquid as possible, and measure to 6 cups. Scrape the flesh from the peppers and add to the broth.

Make the *salmorreta* sauce according to the instructions, using the 2 reserved tomatoes, skinned and seeded, instead of the tomatoes called for in the *salmorreta* recipe. Keep the broth hot over the lowest heat.

Preheat the oven to 400° F for gas oven, 450° F for electric.

Cut the small shelled shrimp crosswise into halves or thirds. Sprinkle the shelled shrimp, the unshelled extra-large shrimp and squid all over with salt. Heat the oil in a paella pan measuring 17 to 18 inches at its widest point (or in a shallow casserole of a similar size), over 2 burners if necessary. Sauté the unshelled shrimp over medium heat until just cooked through. Set aside.

Add the garlic, shelled shrimp, squid, and parsley to the pan and cook 1 minute or so. Stir in the paprika and 4 tablespoons of the *salmorreta* sauce. Add the rice and coat well with the pan mixture. Pour in the broth, bring to a boil, and boil, stirring and rotating the pan occasionally, until the rice is no longer soupy but sufficient liquid remains to continue cooking the rice approximately 5 minutes. Transfer to the oven and cook, uncovered, for 10–12 minutes in a gas oven, 15–20 minutes electric, until the rice is almost al dente. Remove to a warm spot, arrange the large shrimp over the rice, cover with foil, and let sit 5–10 minutes, until the rice is cooked to taste.

Pass the sauce separately and use with the rice and as a dip for the large shrimp.

Rosemary-Scented Shellfish and Egg Paella

(Arroz con Marisco y Huevo al Romero)

Shrimp, squid, clams, and mussels make up the seafood component of this paella, while hard-boiled eggs combine with the rice and also make an attractive garnish before serving. Rosemary, an herb that grows prolifically in Spain's hot Mediterranean climate, is often added to paellas and somehow is the perfect flavor enhancer for paellas such as this one.

Serves 4

- ½ pound Manila clams or cockles, or 1 dozen very small littleneck clams, cleansed (page 10)
- 2 hard-boiled eggs
- 3 cups bottled clam juice or Fish Broth (page 208)
- ⅛ teaspoon crumbled thread saffron
- ½ pound small to medium shrimp, shelled
- ½ pound cleaned squid, in ½-inch rings, tentacles cut in half
- Kosher or sea salt
- 4 tablespoons olive oil
- 2 cloves garlic, minced
- 1 small onion, finely chopped
- 1 medium green bell pepper, finely chopped
- 1 tablespoon chopped fresh rosemary leaves or ½ teaspoon dried, crumbled
- 1 small tomato, finely chopped
- 1 tablespoon minced parsley
- ¼ teaspoon sweet paprika, preferably Spanish smoked
- 1½ cups imported Spanish or Arborio short-grain rice
- 2 medium to large scallions, trimmed and finely chopped
- 12 snap peas or snow peas, strings removed
- 1 jarred pimiento, cut in ½-inch strips
- 6 very small mussels, cleansed (page 10)
- Rosemary sprigs (optional)

If using littleneck clams, place them in ¼ cup of boiling water until they have opened and use any resulting pan liquid as part of the broth to cook the rice. Reserve the clams, covered.

Coarsely chop half of one hard-boiled egg. Slice the rest of the eggs and reserve.

Combine the clam juice and saffron in a pot and keep hot over the lowest heat.

Preheat the oven to 400° F for gas oven, 450° F for electric.

Sprinkle the shrimp and squid all over with salt and let sit at room temperature for 10 minutes. Heat the oil in a paella pan measuring about 13 inches at its widest point (or in a shallow casserole of a similar size). Sauté the shrimp and squid over high heat, turning, for about 1 minute (they should not be fully cooked). Remove to a warm platter. Add the garlic, onion, green pepper, and 1½ teaspoons of the fresh rosemary (¼ teaspoon of the dried). Lower the heat to medium and continue cooking until the pepper is slightly softened, about 3 minutes. Add the tomato and parsley, and cook another 1–2 minutes.

Stir in the paprika, then add the rice, coating well with the pan mixture. Pour in all the hot broth, bring to a boil, and boil for about 2 minutes, stirring. Taste for salt, add the shrimp, squid, and clams (if using Manilas or cockles), chopped egg, and scallions. Continue to boil, stirring occasionally, until the rice is no longer soupy but sufficient liquid remains to continue cooking the rice, about another 3 minutes. Stir in the snap peas and arrange the pimiento and mussels attractively on top.

Transfer to the oven and cook, uncovered, until the rice is almost al dente, 10–12 minutes in a gas oven, 15–20 minutes electric. Remove to a warm spot, arrange the littleneck clams (if used) on top, and scatter with the sliced egg. Cover with foil, and let sit 5–10 minutes, until the rice is cooked to taste. Sprinkle with the remaining rosemary and garnish with the rosemary sprigs, if you wish, before serving.

Golden Rice with Shrimp and Fresh Tuna

(Arroz con Langostinos y Atún)

The golden color and the delicious, characteristic flavor this rice acquires are due to the dried red peppers in this recipe (similar results can be achieved by using fresh red peppers and paprika). Made in the style of the eastern Spanish province of Alicante, this paella does not have many tropezones *(bits and pieces) in the rice, but every time you bite into some shrimp or tuna, the rice bursts with extra flavor. Paellas like this one that have few chunky ingredients are ideally accompanied by an* alioli *sauce. The recipe is adapted from a paella served at the Delfín Restaurant in the capital city of Alicante.*

Serves 4

½ pound small to medium shrimp
    in their shells
4 cups clam juice or Fish Broth
    (page 208)
Alioli (page 211) or Mock Alioli
    (page 213)
8 extra-large shrimp in their
    shells
¾ pound fresh tuna, cut in
    ¾-inch pieces
Kosher or sea salt
7 tablespoons olive oil
17 cloves garlic, peeled
2 teaspoons minced parsley

2 dried sweet red peppers (*ñoras*; see
    Sources, page 215) or mild New
    Mexico peppers, or 1 fresh red bell
    pepper, stem and seeds removed,
    broken or cut into several pieces
¼ teaspoon crumbled thread saffron
2 medium tomatoes, skinned,
    seeded, and finely chopped
1 teaspoon paprika (increase to
    2 tablespoons if using fresh red
    bell pepper)
1¾ cups imported Spanish or
    Arborio short-grain rice
1 pimiento, cut in ½-inch strips

Shell the small or medium shrimp and combine the shells with the clam juice in a pot. Simmer for 20 minutes, then strain and measure to 3½ cups.

Meanwhile, make the *alioli* and transfer to a serving bowl.

Chop the shelled shrimp coarsely. Sprinkle these shrimp, along with the jumbo shrimp in their shells and the tuna, all over with salt and let sit at room temperature. Combine in a cup 1 tablespoon of the oil, 1 clove garlic that has been mashed to a paste, and the parsley. Brush over the tuna. Peel 8 of the remaining cloves garlic and mince the other 8.

Heat 1 tablespoon oil in a small skillet, add the dried red pepper and whole garlic cloves, and sauté 1–2 minutes over low to medium heat, until the peppers are slightly softened and the garlic is very lightly browned. Chop the peppers finely and transfer to a mortar or miniprocessor. Add the sautéed garlic cloves and saffron, and mash to a paste. Stir in the tomato and paprika.

Keep the broth hot over the lowest heat. Preheat the oven to 400° F for a gas oven, 450° F for electric.

Heat the remaining 5 tablespoons oil in a paella pan measuring 13 inches at its widest point (or in a shallow casserole of a similar size) and quickly sear the tuna and large shrimp in their shells. Remove the tuna and shrimp to a warm platter (they should not be fully cooked). Lower the heat to medium, add the chopped shrimp and minced garlic, and sauté a few seconds. Add the rice, stir to coat with the pan mixture, and sauté 2 minutes, stirring frequently.

Add the tomato mixture to the rice and cook 1 minute, then pour in all the hot broth. Bring to a boil, taste for salt, and continue boiling, stirring frequently, until the rice is no longer soupy but sufficient liquid remains to continue cooking the rice, about 5 minutes. Stir in the tuna and attractively arrange the whole shrimp and the pimiento strips over the rice.

Transfer to the oven and cook, uncovered, until the rice is almost al dente, 10–12 minutes in a gas oven, 15–20 minutes electric. Remove to a warm spot, cover with foil, and let sit 5–10 minutes, until the rice is cooked to taste. Serve, passing the *alioli* separately.

Pesto Shellfish Paella

(Paella de Marisco con Puré de Basílico)

A unique paella indeed, using typical Mediterranean ingredients to make a pesto sauce, which gives the rice its remarkable flavor. Mild-tasting shellfish—scallops, clams, and shrimp—balance the robust flavor of the rice.

Try to use cockles, Manila, or other tiny clams if possible; they can be combined with the rice and will open as the rice cooks. Otherwise, use very small littlenecks, cooked as described below. The recipe for the pesto sauce makes twice as much as you will need for this recipe. Use the rest to make Green and Yellow Squash Paella with Pesto (page 146) or save for some other use.

Serves 4

1 dozen extra-large shrimp in their shells
½ pound bay scallops or sea scallops cut in ¾-inch pieces
Kosher or sea salt
4 tablespoons Pesto Sauce (page 210)
3 cups clam juice or Fish Broth (page 208)
⅛ teaspoon crumbled thread saffron
4 tablespoons olive oil
2 tablespoons pine nuts
4 tablespoons finely chopped onion

3 ounces oyster or other mild-flavored mushrooms, brushed clean, stems trimmed, and coarsely chopped (about 1 cup)
1 long, thin, hot green pepper, finely chopped (about 2–3 tablespoons)
3 tablespoons finely chopped tomato
1½ cups imported Spanish or Arborio short-grain rice
½ pound cockles or Manila clams, or 1½ dozen very small littlenecks, cleansed (page 10)
2 tablespoons minced parsley

Sprinkle the shrimp and scallops all over with salt. Let sit for 10 minutes at room temperature. Prepare the Pesto Sauce as directed. If using littleneck clams, place them in ¼ cup of boiling water until they have opened, and use any resulting pan liquid as part of the broth to cook the rice. Reserve the clams and cover.

Combine the clam juice and saffron in a pot and keep hot over the lowest heat.

Preheat the oven to 400° F for gas oven, 450° F for electric.

Heat the oil in a paella pan measuring 13 inches at its widest point (or in a shallow casserole of a similar size). Sauté the shrimp and scallops over high heat for 1–2 minutes (they should not be fully cooked) and remove to a warm platter. Stir in the pine nuts and brown lightly. Add the onion, mushrooms, and hot green pepper, and sauté until the onion is slightly softened. Add the tomato and cook about 2 minutes more.

Stir in the rice and coat it well with the pan mixture. Pour in the broth and bring to a boil, then stir in the pesto sauce and taste for salt. Add the scallops and clams and any juices from the platter, and continue to boil about 5 minutes, until the rice is no longer soupy but sufficient liquid remains to continue cooking the rice. Arrange the shrimp over the rice and transfer to the oven. Cook, uncovered, until the rice is almost al dente, 10–12 minutes in a gas oven, 15–20 minutes electric.

Remove to a warm spot (if using littlenecks, arrange them on top), cover with foil, and let sit 5–10 minutes, until the rice is cooked to taste. Sprinkle with the parsley before serving.

Soupy Rice with Shellfish

(Arroz Caldoso de Marisco)

This is not in truth a paella but another kind of rice dish from the Valencia region that is not as dry as a paella and yet not as fluid as a soup. It is, however, scented with saffron and filled with seafood just like a paella.

If you prepare the broth in advance, all you need to do at the last minute is add the rice and incorporate the seafood. Don't overlook the alioli *toast—it adds immeasurably to the great taste of this rice.*

Serves 4

4 cups bottled clam juice or Fish
    Broth (page 208)
¼ pound medium shrimp in their
    shells
¼ pound bay scallops or sea
    scallops cut in half
1 pound monkfish or grouper, skin
    removed and cut in ¾-inch
    pieces
Kosher or sea salt
2 tablespoons minced parsley
2 cloves garlic, mashed to a paste in
    a mortar or garlic press
¼ cup dry white wine
1 tablespoon lemon juice
1½ teaspoons thyme leaves or
    ¼ teaspoon dried
1 medium leek, very well washed
¼ teaspoon crumbled thread saffron

1 bay leaf
2 sprigs parsley
6 peppercorns
Twelve ¼- to ⅜-inch bread slices
    cut from a long, narrow loaf
2 tablespoons olive oil, plus oil to
    brush the bread
1 small onion, slivered
2 cloves garlic, minced
1 medium tomato, skinned, seeded,
    and finely chopped
1⅓ cups imported Spanish or
    Arborio short-grain rice
2 dozen small to medium
    mussels, thoroughly cleansed
    (page 10)
2 tablespoons Alioli (page 211) or
    Mock Alioli (page 213)

Combine the clam juice with 5 cups water in a soup pot. Shell the shrimp and add the shells to the broth. In a large bowl, combine the shrimp, scallops, and monkfish. Add salt, minced parsley, mashed garlic, wine, lemon juice, and thyme, and refrigerate until ready to use.

Cut off the green portion of the leek and add to the broth (mince the white part and reserve), along with the saffron, bay leaf, parsley sprigs, peppercorns, and salt to taste. Bring to a boil, cover, and simmer 20 minutes. Strain and measure to 8 cups.

To make the toast, brush the bread on both sides with olive oil and bake in a 350° F oven, about 5 minutes, until crusty but not brown, turning once. In a shallow casserole, heat the 2 tablespoons oil and sauté the onion, minced garlic, and minced leek until the vegetables are softened. Add the tomato, cook 3 minutes, then add the reserved broth. Bring to a boil, cover, and simmer about 10 minutes.

Add the rice, return to a boil, and simmer, uncovered, until the rice is almost al dente, 12–15 minutes. Add more liquid if desired (the mixture should have the consistency of a thick soup). Stir in the marinated fish (with any remaining liquid) and the mussels in their shells. Cook 4 minutes, stirring occasionally. Cover and let sit 5 minutes.

Serve in wide, shallow soup bowls. Place a dollop of *alioli* on each piece of toast. Just before eating, float a piece of toast in each bowl of soup; otherwise the bread will turn soggy.

Garlicky Clam Paella

(Arroz de Almejas a la Marinera)

Clams are the main feature of this paella—chopped up in the rice and in their shells over the rice. Since most clams (except for tiny Manilas and cockles) are sold by the dozen, buy large ones for chopping (that way you will get the most meat) and smaller ones to leave in their shells. The rice is well seasoned with garlic, parsley, and onion—perfect and typically Spanish complements to the clams.

Serves 4

1 dozen large littleneck clams, cleansed (page 10)

8 cloves garlic, minced

⅛ teaspoon crumbled thread saffron

8 tablespoons minced parsley

Kosher or sea salt

¼ cup dry white wine

2 teaspoons lemon juice

4 tablespoons olive oil

½ cup minced onion

¼ cup well-washed, minced leeks (white part only)

1 small green bell pepper, finely chopped

1 bay leaf

One 1-inch piece dried red chile pepper or ¼ teaspoon crushed red pepper

¼ teaspoon sweet paprika, preferably Spanish smoked

1½ cups imported Spanish or Arborio short-grain rice

24–32 Manila clams or cockles, or 12–18 very small littleneck clams, cleansed (page 10)

Place the large clams (and small littlenecks if using) in a skillet with 3 cups water. Bring to a boil, cover, and cook, removing the clams as they open. Chop the meat from the large clams finely (cover the small littlenecks and reserve). Measure the broth to 2¾ cups.

In a mortar or miniprocessor, mash to a paste the garlic, saffron, 6 tablespoons of the parsley, and ⅛ teaspoon salt. Stir in the wine and lemon juice. Keep the clam broth hot over the lowest heat.

Preheat the oven to 400° F for gas oven, 450° F for electric.

Heat the oil in a paella pan measuring about 13 inches at its widest point (or in a shallow casserole of a similar size) and slowly sauté the onion, leeks, pepper, bay leaf, and chile pepper until the vegetables are softened. Add the chopped clams and sauté 5 minutes more. Remove the bay leaf and chile pepper, and stir in the paprika. Add the rice and coat well with the pan mixture. Pour in the broth, bring to a boil, taste for salt, add the mortar mixture and Manila clams, and boil, stirring occasionally, for about 5 minutes, until the rice is no longer soupy but sufficient liquid remains to continue cooking the rice. Transfer to the oven and cook, uncovered, 10–12 minutes in a gas oven, 15–20 minutes electric, until the rice is almost al dente.

Remove to a warm spot (if using littlenecks, arrange them over the rice). Cover with foil, and let sit 5–10 minutes, until the rice is cooked to taste. Sprinkle with the remaining 2 tablespoons parsley and serve.

Mussel Paella

(Paella de Mejillones)

A simple paella that relies almost entirely on mussels for its superb flavor. Mussels are typically little more than decorative notes to a seafood paella, but here they are the star attraction.

The amount of mussels may seem excessive, but keep in mind that about half are chopped and will blend into the rice, while the rest will garnish the paella and be eaten from the shell.

Serves 6 to 8

6 pounds mussels, preferably small cultivated mussels, cleansed (page 10)

⅔ cup dry white wine

About 5¼ cups clam juice or Fish Broth (page 108)

¼ teaspoon crumbled thread saffron

1 tablespoon thyme leaves or ½ teaspoon dried

1 tablespoon chopped rosemary leaves or ½ teaspoon dried

¼ cup freshly squeezed lemon juice

8 tablespoons olive oil

1 medium onion, finely chopped

8 cloves garlic, minced

2 tablespoons minced shallots

4 tablespoons minced parsley

4 pimientos, 2 chopped and 2 cut in ½-inch strips

3 cups imported Spanish or Arborio short-grain rice

Salt

Freshly ground pepper to taste

Put aside 6–10 mussels per person, depending on size. Pour the wine into a large skillet, add the remaining mussels, cover, and bring to a boil. Cook over high heat, removing the mussels to a plate as they open. Reserve the broth that remains in the skillet and combine it with enough clam juice to make 6 cups. Add the saffron, thyme, rosemary, and lemon juice. Keep hot over the lowest heat. Remove the mussel meat from the open shells, chop coarsely, and set aside. Discard the shells.

Preheat the oven to 400° F for gas oven, 450° F for electric.

Heat the oil in a paella pan measuring 17–18 inches at its widest point (or in a shallow casserole of a similar size), over 2 burners if necessary. Add the onion, garlic, shallots, and parsley. Stir in the chopped mussel meat and the chopped pimientos. Cook 1 minute, then add the rice and coat well with the pan mixture. Pour in all the hot broth and bring to a boil. Taste for salt and season with pepper. Continue to boil, stirring and rotating the pan occasionally, until the rice is no longer soupy but sufficient liquid remains to continue cooking the rice, about 5 minutes.

Arrange the pimiento strips and the reserved unopened mussels attractively over the rice, with the edge of the mussels that are open facing up. Transfer to the oven and cook, uncovered, until the rice is almost al dente, 10–12 minutes in a gas oven, 15–20 minutes electric. Remove to a warm spot, cover with foil, and let sit 5–10 minutes, until the rice is cooked to taste.

Lobster Paella "Casa Roberto"

(Paella de Langosta "Casa Roberto")

In times past an elegant restaurant in Valencia called Los Viveros was celebrated for its lobster paella. Lobster is a luxury item in Spain; its price is in the stratosphere, and it is seldom used in paella. So it was fitting that a deluxe restaurant would be the one serving this paella.

Recently I discovered Casa Roberto, a restaurant in the city of Valencia that carries on the tradition. A cozy, casual establishment, it was not the setting I had expected for this rare paella. After placing my order I proceeded to the kitchen to join chef Juanjo and watch an expert at work.

Of course, paellas made in restaurants by chefs that do little else is a simpler operation than making them in the home kitchen: the burners are large to accommodate oversized paella pans, all the ingredients are chopped and at hand, nothing is measured (each chef has his method of calculating the proper amount of liquid), and there is always a stockpot simmering on a back burner. Nevertheless, there were tricks to be learned.

The cost of putting live lobster over a paella and also using lobster meat in the rice would make an already expensive dish even more so. Instead, poor man's lobster—monkfish—is incorporated into the rice for a lobsterlike taste and texture. The split lobsters, of course, also lend their flavor to the paella while providing a spectacular appearance and lots of pleasurable eating. Live lobster is best, of course (and its tommaley—the green liver—adds flavor to the broth), but frozen lobster tails may be substituted.

Serves 6

6½ cups clam juice or Fish Broth (page 208)

1 medium onion, finely chopped

Three 1¼- to 1½-pound live lobsters, split, or 6 defrosted lobster tails

4 cloves garlic, minced

1 large red bell pepper, finely chopped

¼ teaspoon crumbled thread saffron

2 tablespoons finely chopped cooked carrot

1½ teaspoons thyme leaves or ¼ teaspoon dried

4 tablespoons minced parsley

1 bay leaf

1 medium tomato, skinned, seeded, and finely chopped

1 pound monkfish, cut in ½-inch cubes

1 teaspoon sweet paprika, preferably Spanish smoked

Kosher or sea salt

3 cups imported Spanish or Arborio short-grain rice

8 tablespoons olive oil

½ cup frozen or fresh peas

Separate the tail sections and claws from the lobsters. Combine in a pot the clam juice with the lobster heads and legs, saffron, thyme, and bay leaf. Bring to a boil and simmer 30 minutes. Strain and measure to 6 cups. Keep hot over the lowest heat.

Preheat the oven to 400° F for gas oven, 450° F for electric. Sprinkle the monkfish all over with salt.

Heat 6 tablespoons of the oil in a paella pan measuring 17–18 inches at its widest point (or in a shallow casserole of a similar size), over 2 burners if necessary. Sauté the lobster over high heat, turning once, about 1 minute to each side (it will not be fully cooked). Remove to a warm platter. Add the monkfish to the pan, sauté 1 minute, and remove to the platter.

Lower the heat to medium-high, add the remaining oil, and sauté the onion, garlic, pepper, carrot, and 2 tablespoons of the parsley until the onion is slightly softened. Add the tomato and cook 2 minutes. Stir in the paprika, then the rice, and sauté 1 minute, coating well with the pan mixture. Pour in all the hot broth (discard the bay leaf) and bring to a boil. Taste for salt and boil 2 minutes.

Return the monkfish and any liquid on the platter to the pan, add the peas, and boil for about 3 minutes more, stirring and rotating the pan occasionally, until the rice is no longer soupy but sufficient liquid remains to continue cooking the rice. Arrange the lobster over the rice, transfer to the oven, and cook, uncovered, until the rice is almost al dente, 10–12 minutes in a gas oven, 15–20 minutes electric. Remove to a warm spot, cover with foil, and let sit 5–10 minutes, until the rice is cooked to taste. Return the paella to the stove over high heat until a crust of rice forms at the bottom of the pan (be careful not to burn).

Crabmeat Paella with Peas

(Paella de Centolla con Guisantes)

Make this excellent paella with cooked lump crabmeat that you will find in fish markets, fresh or frozen (just be sure it is pure crabmeat, not the mix of crab, fish, and flavorings that often passes for crab). You can also include crabs in their shells, crab claws, or crab legs for a pretty presentation and for the pleasure of cracking them open and extracting the sweet morsels of meat.

In Spain this paella is made from centolla, the large spider crab found off the northern coast, but other crabmeats will do fine. If you buy small live blue crabs, for example, boil them (use the broth for the rice), split them in half crosswise, remove the tomalley (green liver) and any roe, and add the liver and roe to the paella broth; it will give an uncommonly rich flavor.

Serves 6 to 8

8 cloves garlic, minced

4 tablespoons minced parsley

1 tablespoon thyme leaves or
　½ teaspoon dried

½ teaspoon crushed red pepper

1 bay leaf, crumbled

Kosher or sea salt

6-ounce can flaked crabmeat

¼ teaspoon crumbled thread
　saffron

About 5¾ cups clam juice or Fish
　Broth (page 208)

8 tablespoons olive oil

1 medium onion, finely chopped

6 tablespoons well-washed minced
　leeks (white part only)

2 small green frying peppers
　("Italian") or 1 medium green
　bell pepper, finely chopped

2 medium tomatoes, skinned,
　seeded, and finely chopped

½ cup finely chopped cooked
　carrot

¼ cup brandy

½ teaspoon sweet paprika,
　preferably Spanish smoked

3 cups imported Spanish or
　Arborio short-grain rice

2 tablespoons freshly squeezed
　lemon juice

1 cup frozen or fresh peas

1 pound fresh or frozen cooked
　lump crabmeat, picked over

Cooked crab in its shell, such as
　whole blue crab, Alaskan king
　crab legs, or stone crab claws
　(optional)

In a mortar or miniprocessor, mash to a paste 4 cloves garlic, the parsley, thyme, crushed red pepper, bay leaf, and ¼ teaspoon salt. (Add and mash any roe or tomalley if using live crabs.) Drain the liquid from the canned crabmeat and combine in a pot with the saffron and enough broth to make 6 cups. Keep hot over the lowest heat.

Preheat the oven to 400° F for gas oven, 450° F for electric.

Heat the oil in a paella pan measuring 17–18 inches at its widest point (or in a shallow casserole of a similar size), over 2 burners if necessary. Add the onion, the leeks and peppers, and remaining 4 cloves garlic and sauté slowly until the vegetables are softened. Stir in the tomatoes, cooked carrot, and brandy and boil away the liquid over high heat. Stir in the paprika and rice, coating it well with the pan mixture. Pour in all the broth and the lemon juice and bring to a boil. Add the mortar mixture and peas, taste for salt, and continue to boil, stirring and rotating the pan occasionally, until the rice is no longer soupy but sufficient liquid remains to continue cooking the rice. Stir in the crabmeat, arrange the optional crab in its shell over the rice, transfer to the oven, and cook, uncovered, until the rice is almost al dente, 10–12 minutes in a gas oven, 15–20 minutes electric.

Remove to a warm spot, cover with foil, and let sit 5–10 minutes, until the rice is cooked to taste.

Stewed Squid Paella "El Faro"
(Arroz con Chocos "El Faro")

From my good friend Gonzalo Córdoba, owner of El Faro, the finest restaurant in the Andalusian city of Cádiz, comes this truly exceptional rice—succulent, full of flavor, and with a captivating hint of sweetness that is a result of the Andalusian touch of medium-sweet sherry and of slow-cooking the squid and onion before combining them with the rice. Although stewing the squid before making the paella adds time, it does not involve any extra work.

Andalucía may not be authentic paella country, but El Faro's squid paella would, I think, bring even Valencians to their knees.

Serves 6 to 8

8 tablespoons olive oil

2 bread slices, ¼–⅜ inch thick, cut from a long, narrow loaf

3 medium onions, finely chopped

2 bay leaves

2 pounds cleaned squid with tentacles, cut in a 1-inch dice and tentacles halved lengthwise

2 tablespoons dry white wine

Kosher or sea salt

10 cloves garlic, finely chopped

¼ teaspoon crumbled thread saffron

2 tablespoons minced parsley

2 tablespoons *oloroso* (medium-sweet) sherry or medium-sweet white wine

6 cups clam juice or Fish Broth (page 208)

½ large red bell pepper, finely chopped

1 large green bell pepper, finely chopped

3 cups imported Spanish or Arborio short-grain rice

Heat 2 tablespoons of the oil in a large, shallow casserole and sauté the bread slices, turning once, until brown. Remove and drain on paper towels. Add to the casserole two-thirds of the chopped onions and the bay leaves, and sauté for 2 minutes. Add the squid and sauté 1 minute more. Stir in the white wine and salt to taste. Cover and simmer until the squid is tender, about 30 minutes.

Meanwhile, soak the sautéed bread in water and squeeze dry. In a mortar or miniprocessor mash to a paste the bread, garlic, saffron, parsley, and ¼ teaspoon salt. Stir in the *oloroso* sherry. When the squid is cooked, add the mortar mixture and cook 10 minutes more, uncovered.

Keep the clam juice hot over the lowest heat. Preheat the oven to 400° F for gas oven, 450° F for electric.

Heat the remaining 6 tablespoons oil in a paella pan measuring 17–18 inches at its widest point (or a shallow casserole of a similar size), over 2 burners if necessary, and sauté the red and green peppers and remaining chopped onion over medium-high heat until the peppers are slightly softened. Stir in the rice and coat well with the pan mixture. Add the stewed squid and pour in the hot broth. Bring to a boil, taste for salt, and continue to boil, stirring and rotating the pan occasionally if over 2 burners, until the rice is no longer soupy but sufficient liquid remains to continue cooking the rice, about 5 minutes.

Transfer to the oven and cook, uncovered, until the rice is almost al dente, 10–12 minutes in a gas oven, 15–20 minutes electric. Remove to a warm spot, cover with foil, and let sit 5–10 minutes, until the rice is cooked to taste.

Black Squid Paella

(Arroz Negro)

This is one of the paella greats, so extraordinary that it eclipses most other paellas. It is almost jet black—colored and flavored by squid ink—and filled with tidbits of squid, shrimp, and monkfish. Arroz negro is served with alioli—a wonderful addition of flavor and a contrast in color and texture. (If possible, make your own; with a food processor it takes just five minutes.) A visually stunning dish with a memorable taste that wows everyone who tries it.

Removing enough squid ink from the sacs of fresh uncleaned squid is a messy and thankless job. Instead, plan ahead and buy vacuum packets of ink (see Sources, page 215) by mail order. They are inexpensive and will keep for months in the freezer; I always have a supply on hand. To enrich the broth, add the shrimp shells and fish scraps and simmer 20 minutes. Strain and measure to 6 cups.

Serves 6 to 8

Alioli (page 211) or Mock Alioli (page 213)

½ pound medium shrimp, shelled

½ pound monkfish, grouper, or other firm-fleshed fish, skin removed and cut in ½-inch cubes

2 pounds small cleaned squid (including tentacles), cut in ½-inch rings and tentacles halved lengthwise

Kosher or sea salt

8 cloves garlic, minced

2 tablespoons minced parsley

Six 4-gram packets squid ink

6 cups clam juice or Fish Broth (page 208)

¼ teaspoon crumbled thread saffron

2 tablespoons freshly squeezed lemon juice

8 tablespoons olive oil

1 medium onion, finely chopped

2 medium red bell peppers, finely chopped

2 medium tomatoes, finely chopped

2 teaspoons sweet paprika, preferably Spanish smoked

3 cups imported Spanish or Arborio short-grain rice

4 frozen artichoke hearts in quarters

1 large pimiento, cut in ½-inch strips

Lemon wedges

Make the *alioli* according to the instructions and transfer to a serving bowl. Sprinkle the shrimp, monkfish, and squid all over with salt and let sit 10 minutes at room temperature. Mash to paste in a mortar or miniprocessor half of the minced garlic, the parsley, and ⅛ teaspoon salt. Stir in the squid ink and reserve.

Combine the clam juice with the saffron and lemon juice. Keep hot over the lowest heat.

Preheat the oven to 400° F for gas ovens, 450° F for electric.

Heat 2 tablespoons of the oil in a paella pan measuring 17–18 inches at its widest point (or in a shallow casserole of a similar size), over 2 burners if necessary, and sauté the shrimp, monkfish, and squid over high heat for 1–2 minutes (they should not be fully cooked). Remove to a warm platter. Add the remaining 2 tablespoons oil, the onion and red peppers, and sauté over medium-high heat until the onion is lightly browned. Stir in the tomatoes and the remaining minced garlic, sauté 1–2 minutes, then stir in the paprika. Add the rice and coat well with the pan mixture. Pour in the broth and bring to a boil. Add the mortar mixture and the artichokes, and taste for salt. Continue to boil, stirring and rotating the pan occasionally, about 2 minutes. Stir in the reserved shrimp, monkfish, squid, and any juices from the platter, and boil until the rice is no longer soupy but sufficient liquid remains to continue cooking the rice, about 5 minutes.

Arrange the pimiento strips attractively over the rice and transfer to the oven. Cook 10–12 minutes in a gas oven, 15–20 minutes electric, until the rice is almost al dente. Remove to a warm spot, cover with foil, and let sit, until the rice is cooked to taste. Arrange lemon wedges around the edge of the pan before serving. Pass the *alioli* separately.

Squid and Scallion Paella

(Arroz de Chipirones y Ajos Tiernos)

Squid is an exceedingly popular ingredient in seafood paellas as well as in mixed meat and seafood paellas. Here the squid stands alone, enhanced by a goodly amount of scallions.

The rice is cooked in a broth flavored with either dried red pepper or lots of paprika, and is served with alioli *sauce on the side.*

Serves 6

6 cups clam juice or Fish Broth (page 208)

¼ teaspoon crumbled thread saffron

1 pound (about 4 bunches) scallions, trimmed and chopped

1½ pounds cleaned squid, cut in ½-inch rings, tentacles cut in half lengthwise

8 tablespoons olive oil

8 cloves garlic, peeled, and 4 cloves garlic, minced

3 sweet dried red peppers (*ñoras*; see Sources, page 215) or 2 mild New Mexico dried red peppers, cored and seeded, or 1 fresh red bell pepper, finely chopped

3 medium tomatoes, coarsely chopped

2 teaspoons sweet paprika, preferably Spanish smoked (increase to 2 tablespoons if using fresh red pepper instead of dried)

Salt

Alioli (page 211) or Mock Alioli (page 213)

½ cup dry white wine

3 cups imported Spanish or Arborio short-grain rice

Combine the clam juice, saffron, half of the scallions, and any squid scraps in a pot. Heat 3 tablespoons of the oil in a paella pan measuring 17–18 inches at its widest point (or in a shallow casserole of a similar size), over 2 burners if necessary. Sauté the garlic cloves and red peppers over medium heat about 2 minutes (be careful not to burn). Add them to the broth. Add the tomatoes, sauté 1–2 minutes and stir in the paprika. Transfer the tomato mixture to the broth and wipe out the paella pan. Bring the broth to a boil, season with salt, cover, and simmer 30 minutes.

Meanwhile, make the *alioli* and transfer to a serving bowl. Sprinkle the squid all over with salt and let sit at room temperature. Strain the broth, pressing with the back of a wooden spoon to extract as much liquid from the remaining solid pieces as possible. Reserve 5½ cups of the broth, combine with the wine, and keep hot over the lowest heat.

Preheat the oven to 400° F for gas oven, 450° F for electric.

Heat the remaining 5 tablespoons oil in the paella pan and sauté the squid over high heat about 1 minute. Remove to a warm platter. Lower the heat to medium, add the remaining scallions and the minced garlic, and sauté another 1–2 minutes. Add the rice and coat well with the pan mixture. Sauté 1–2 minutes. Pour in all the hot broth and bring to a boil. Taste for salt and continue to boil, stirring and rotating the pan occasionally, about 5 minutes, until the rice is no longer soupy but sufficient liquid remains to continue cooking the rice. Stir in the squid.

Transfer to the oven and cook, uncovered, until the rice is almost al dente, 10–12 minutes in a gas oven, 15–20 minutes electric. Remove to a warm spot, cover with foil, and let sit 5–10 minutes, until the rice is cooked to taste. Pass the *alioli* separately.

Mixed Seafood Paella

(Arroz a la Marinera)

In Spain a mixed seafood paella is the one you will find most Spaniards enjoying in summer at restaurants by the sea and at the ever-popular beach lean-tos called chiringuitos. *I think this version is the best I have ever eaten. It requires firm fish that will not fall apart when cooked (both monkfish and grouper fit the bill) and a well-flavored cooking liquid enriched with fish scraps, mussel broth, and a mash of garlic, parsley, and thyme.*

Serves 6

3 dozen small to medium mussels, thoroughly cleansed (page 10)

About 5½ cups clam juice or Fish Broth (page 208)

¼ teaspoon crumbled thread saffron

¾ pound monkfish or other firm-fleshed fish, skin removed and cut in ½-inch cubes

¾ pound grouper or other firm-fleshed fish, cut in ½-inch cubes

1 pound small cleaned squid with tentacles, cut in ½-inch dice and tentacles halved lengthwise

18 large shrimp in their shells

Kosher or sea salt

2 tablespoons minced parsley

8 cloves garlic, minced

1 tablespoon thyme leaves or ½ teaspoon dried

2 teaspoons sweet paprika, preferably Spanish smoked

8 tablespoons olive oil

1 medium onion, finely chopped

6 small scallions, green portion trimmed, finely chopped

2 red bell peppers, finely chopped

1 medium tomato, finely chopped

3 cups imported Spanish or Arborio short-grain rice

Place 1½ dozen mussels in a skillet with ¾ cup water. Cover and bring to a boil. Remove the mussels as they open. Reserve the meat and discard the shells. When all the mussels have opened, pour the liquid from the skillet into a large pot and add enough clam juice to make 6 cups. Stir in the saffron.

Dry the monkfish, grouper, squid, and shrimp well between paper towels. Sprinkle all over with salt and let sit 10 minutes at room temperature. In a mortar or miniprocessor, mash to a paste the parsley, garlic, thyme, and ⅛ teaspoon salt. Stir in the paprika and a little water if necessary to form a paste.

Keep the broth hot over the lowest heat. Preheat the oven to 400° F for gas oven, 450° F for electric.

Heat 6 tablespoons of the oil in a paella pan measuring 17–18 inches at its widest point (or in a shallow casserole of a similar size), over 2 burners if necessary. Quickly sauté the monkfish, grouper, squid, and shrimp (in their shells) 1–2 minutes (they should not be fully cooked). Remove the seafood to a warm platter. Add the remaining 2 tablespoons oil, the onion, scallions, and red peppers, and cook over medium-high heat until the vegetables are slightly softened. Raise the heat, add the tomato, and cook about 2 minutes.

Stir in the rice and coat well with the pan mixture. Pour in all the hot broth and bring to a boil. Continue to boil for about 3 minutes, stirring and rotating the pan occasionally. Add all the reserved fish (except the shrimp), the reserved mussel meat, and the mortar mixture. Taste for salt and continue to boil about 2 minutes more, until the rice is no longer soupy but sufficient liquid remains to continue cooking the rice.

Arrange the shrimp and the uncooked mussels over the rice, placing the edge of the mussel shells that will open facing up. Transfer to the oven and cook, uncovered, until the rice is almost al dente, 10–12 minutes in a gas oven, 15–20 minutes electric. Remove to a warm spot (if most of the liquid has not been absorbed, place the pan over high heat for 1–2 minutes without stirring), then cover with foil and let sit 5–10 minutes, until the rice is cooked to taste.

"Rice on Its Own" El Pegolí

(Arroz a Banda El Pegolí)

I wouldn't dream of visiting the Valencia region without stopping at El Pegolí, overlooking the Mediterranean near the town of Denia in the province of Alicante. There are no menus here—everyone is eating exactly the same simple, exquisite fare: a glistening fresh salad, just-caught boiled shellfish of a quality beyond compare, and the pièce de résistance, arroz a banda, *literally "rice all by itself." Owner Pepe Piera, tall and as thin as a reed, takes charge of the dining room in his amusingly dictatorial fashion, although he is really soft-hearted beneath his sometimes severe countenance. Nostalgic for the old days, he fills the restaurant with portraits and photographs of his parents, who started the restaurant many decades ago, and with signed photographs of politicians, bullfighters, and other celebrities, past and present.*

His wife and daughter control the cooking at El Pegolí, and I ducked into the kitchen to get more details on this recipe that has been in the family for three generations. From the Plain Jane looks of the rice you would never imagine this could be such an extraordinary dish. It is not even presented in a paella pan but is unceremoniously heaped on a plain platter. And you will not find even a morsel of seafood or a vegetable or anything else except rice. But what rice! To me, it is the very quintessence of paella.

The arroz a banda *at El Pegolí begins with* arroz bomba, *a remarkable rice that expands like an accordion when cooked and has a unique texture (see Sources, page 215). Otherwise, the secret to this rice lies entirely in the broth, a slowly simmered brew of fish, garlic, tomato, paprika, and dried sweet red peppers. Here is one paella for which you must make your own broth, because the broth is everything. But once the broth is made, you are home free.*

Also important is the wonderful alioli *that accompanies the rice at El Pegolí; it is made with some boiled potato to cut the bite of the garlic. I suggest a simple seafood before the rice. Boiled and cooled or grilled large shrimp in their shells (which are also great with the* alioli) *are ideal.*

Serves 6

1 pound cleaned squid, with
    tentacles
1 pound cleaned whiting or other
    inexpensive fish
¼ teaspoon crumbled thread
    saffron
1 tablespoon paprika, preferably
    Spanish smoked (add 2 more
    tablespoons if using fresh red
    peppers instead of dried)
Parsley sprigs
Kosher or sea salt
2 cups clam juice
8 tablespoons olive oil

3 dried sweet red peppers (*ñoras*; see
    Sources, page 215), 2 dried mild
    New Mexico peppers, or 1 large
    fresh red bell pepper, cored,
    seeded, and broken or cut into
    several pieces
1 head garlic, divided into cloves
    and peeled
2 medium tomatoes, coarsely
    chopped
Potato Alioli (page 212) or Mock
    Alioli (page 213)
3 cups imported Spanish or
    Arborio short-grain rice

Combine 7 cups water with the squid, whiting, saffron, paprika, parsley, salt to taste, and clam juice. Bring to a boil and keep at a simmer.

In a paella pan measuring 17–18 inches at its widest point (or in a shallow casserole of a similar size), over 2 burners if necessary, heat 3 tablespoons of the oil and sauté the red peppers and the whole garlic cloves over medium heat, until the dried peppers are slightly softened, 1–2 minutes, taking care not to burn. Remove the peppers and garlic and add to the broth (leave the oil in the pan).

Sauté the tomatoes 1–2 minutes and also add to the pot, leaving the oil in the pan. Simmer the broth for about 1 hour. Meanwhile, make the *alioli*.

Remove the squid from the pot and strain the broth, pressing with the back of a wooden spoon to extract as much liquid as possible. Reserve 6 cups of the broth and keep hot over the lowest heat. Mince the squid (this can be done in a food processor).

Preheat the oven to 400° F for gas oven, 450° F for electric.

Heat the remaining 5 tablespoons oil in the paella pan and sauté the squid for 1 minute. Add the rice, coat well with the pan mixture, and sauté 1–2 minutes. Pour in all the hot broth and bring to a boil. Taste for salt. Continue to boil, stirring and rotating the pan occasionally, until the rice is no longer soupy but sufficient liquid remains to continue cooking the rice, about 5 minutes.

Transfer to the oven and cook, uncovered, until the rice is almost al dente, 10–12 minutes in a gas oven, 15–20 minutes electric. Remove to a warm spot, cover with foil, and let sit 5–10 minutes, until the rice is cooked to taste. Serve, passing the potato *alioli* separately.

Seafood Rice, Murcia Style

(Arroz de Caldero Murciano)

Murcia, just south of the Valencia region, also produces rice and is a place where eating rice is a time-honored tradition. Arroz de Caldero is the pride of Murcia, a unique preparation that is not called paella or made in a paella pan. A deep iron pot is used—any heavy pot will work fine—and the consistency is slightly fluid, not as dry as a paella. What is lost in showy presentation is gained in extraordinary flavor.

Like Arroz a Banda (page 48), the flavor depends almost entirely on the richness of the broth, here heavily seasoned with dried red peppers. (You may substitute fresh red pepper and additional paprika, but the taste will not be as subtle.) The fish in the recipe is poached in the broth and served on the side, and both the fish and the rice are accompanied by a marvelous alioli with a strong punch of garlic softened by the addition of potato.

Serves 6

4 tablespoons olive oil

20 medium cloves garlic, peeled

10 sweet dried red peppers (*ñoras*; see Sources, page 215) or 6 mild dried New Mexico peppers, cored and seeded, or 2 red bell peppers, cored and seeded plus 4 tablespoons sweet imported paprika

11 cups clam juice or water

½ cup chopped onion

2 large tomatoes, chopped

1 pound cleaned whiting

¼ teaspoon crumbled thread saffron

Kosher or sea salt

Potato Alioli (page 212) or Mock Alioli (page 213)

One 1-pound piece boneless striped bass or other bluefish, about 1–1½ inches thick, skin on

1½ pounds monkfish of a similar thickness

3 cups imported Spanish or Arborio short-grain rice

In a deep, heavy pot, heat 3 tablespoons of the oil and very slowly sauté the garlic and peppers, turning occasionally, until the garlic is golden and the peppers are slightly softened—be very careful not to burn them. Transfer to a food processor, leaving the oil in the pot, and mince very finely. With the motor running, gradually add 2 cups of the clam juice.

In the oil remaining in the pot, sauté the onion until softened. Add the tomatoes and cook

1 minute, then add the remaining 9 cups clam juice, the whiting, saffron, salt to taste, and the mixture from the food processor. Bring to a boil and simmer, uncovered, 30 minutes. Meanwhile, make the *alioli*.

Strain the broth, pushing through as much of the solid material as possible. Add the striped bass and monkfish, and simmer about 15 minutes, or 10 minutes for each inch of thickness. Remove the fish to a separate pot, barely cover with some of the broth, cover, and keep in a warm spot. Measure the remaining broth to make 9 cups, adding liquid or boiling down the liquid as necessary. Bring the broth to a boil and add the rice. Simmer about 15 minutes, uncovered, or until the rice is almost al dente.

Turn off the heat, cover, and let rest about 5 minutes. Serve the fish and rice on separate plates and pass the *alioli*.

Seafood Pasta Paella

(Fideuá)

Even though this peerless seafood pasta has no rice, it is made in a paella pan like a paella and uses similar ingredients, so I include it in this cookbook. Pasta rarely appears in traditional Spanish cooking except as a soup noodle, but it gains importance on Spain's eastern shore, partly because in the sixteenth and seventeenth centuries Spain and Italy were closely tied. Much of Italy belonged to the Spanish Crown, and Spain's northern Mediterranean ports were important centers of commerce.

Catalunya, north of the Valencia region, has several traditional pasta dishes, such as rossejat de fideus, a crisp pasta with seafood, and meat-filled canelones baked with a white sauce. And the Valencia region has its fideuá, which relies on a pasta similar to perci-atelli that has a narrow hole through its center, allowing all the flavors of the broth to permeate the pasta. A run under the broiler gives it a crisp finish, and the alioli sauce provides a final exquisite touch. I wager this pasta dish is unlike any you have ever eaten and one of the greatest ways to serve pasta.

Serves 6

½ pound small to medium shrimp, shelled, left whole if small, or cut in half crosswise

½ pound monkfish, grouper, or other firm-textured fish, skin removed and cut in ½-inch pieces

½ pound cleaned squid, diced and tentacles cut in half lengthwise

Kosher or sea salt

Alioli (page 211) or Mock Alioli (page 213)

7 cups bottled clam juice or Fish Broth (page 208)

¼ teaspoon crumbled thread saffron

7 tablespoons olive oil

1 green bell pepper, finely chopped

16 cloves garlic, minced

2 medium tomatoes, finely chopped

2 tablespoons minced parsley

½ cup dry white wine

1 pound perciatelli pasta, broken into 1½-inch lengths

2 teaspoons sweet paprika, preferably Spanish smoked

½ teaspoon cayenne pepper

3 dozen tiny clams, such as cockles or Manila, or 1½ dozen very small littlenecks, cleansed (page 10)

2 dozen very small mussels, cleansed (page 10)

Sprinkle the shrimp, monkfish, and squid all over with salt and let sit at room temperature for 10 minutes. Make the *alioli* and transfer to a serving bowl. Combine the broth and saffron in a pot and keep hot over the lowest heat. (If using littlenecks, open them in ¼ cup boiling water and use any liquid as part of the broth.) Remove to a platter, cover and reserve.

Preheat the oven to 400° F for gas oven, 450° F for electric.

Heat the oil in a paella pan measuring 17–18 inches at its widest point (or in a shallow casserole of a similar size), over 2 burners if necessary. Quickly sauté the shrimp, monkfish, and squid over high heat, just until their surface turns opaque, under 1 minute (they should not be fully cooked). Remove to a warm platter. Lower the heat to medium-high and sauté the green pepper until slightly softened, then add the garlic, tomatoes, parsley, and wine. Bring to a boil and continue boiling until the liquid is cooked away.

Add the pasta, stir to coat well with the pan mixture, and sauté for about 2 minutes, stirring constantly. Add the paprika, cayenne, and hot broth. Bring to a boil, taste for salt, and continue boiling, stirring and rotating the pan occasionally, until the pasta is no longer soupy but sufficient liquid remains to continue cooking the pasta, 10–15 minutes.

Return the shrimp, monkfish, and squid to the pan and, if using cockles or Manila clams, stir them in, along with the mussels. Transfer to the oven and cook, uncovered, 7–10 minutes, until the pasta is almost al dente and most of the liquid is absorbed. Remove to a warm spot, cover with foil, and let sit 5 minutes. Uncover and run under the broiler to brown the pasta, about 1½ minutes. (If using littlenecks, arrange them over the rice.) Serve, passing the *alioli* separately.

Monkfish, Swiss Chard, and Sesame Seed Paella

(Paella de Rape, Acelgas, y Sésamo)

A most unusual paella that combines mild-tasting monkfish with slightly pungent Swiss chard and crunchy sesame seeds. Be sure to sprinkle more sesame seeds on the finished rice—it will highlight the rice's nutty flavor.

Serves 4

½ pound monkfish, grouper, or other firm-fleshed fish steaks, skin removed and cut in ½-inch pieces

Kosher or sea salt

¾ pound Swiss chard (weight after trimming), thick stems trimmed

4 tablespoons sesame seeds

6 cloves garlic, minced

3 tablespoons minced parsley

3 cups clam juice or vegetable broth or fish broth, canned or homemade (page 208)

⅛ teaspoon crumbled thread saffron

4 tablespoons olive oil

1 small onion, finely chopped

2 tablespoons minced shallots

1 small tomato, finely chopped

¼ teaspoon sweet paprika, preferably Spanish smoked

1½ cups imported Spanish or Arborio short-grain rice

Preheat the oven to 425° F.

Sprinkle the fish all over with salt. Separate the white stems and green leaves of the Swiss chard. Chop each coarsely. Toast the sesame seeds on a tray in the oven until lightly brown, about 3 minutes. Mash to a paste in a mortar or miniprocessor half of the minced garlic, 2 tablespoons of the parsley, and ⅛ teaspoon salt.

Combine the clam juice with the saffron in a pot and keep hot over the lowest heat. Adjust the oven temperature to 400° F for gas oven, 450° F for electric.

Heat the oil in a paella pan measuring about 13 inches at its widest point (or in a shallow casserole of a similar size) and sauté the fish over high heat, about 1 minute (it should not be fully cooked). Remove to a warm platter.

Lower the heat and sauté the remaining garlic, the onion, shallots, and Swiss chard stems until the vegetables are slightly softened. Add the tomato, cook 1–2 minutes, then stir in the paprika. Add the rice and coat well with the pan mixture. Pour in the hot clam juice and bring to a boil. Add the mortar mixture, taste for salt, and continue to boil, stirring occasionally, until the rice is no longer soupy but sufficient liquid remains to continue cooking the rice, about 5 minutes.

Mix in 2 tablespoons of the sesame seeds, the Swiss chard leaves, and the reserved fish, and transfer to the oven. Cook, uncovered, until the rice is almost al dente, 10–12 minutes in a gas oven, 15–20 minutes electric. Remove to a warm spot, cover with foil, and let sit 5–10 minutes, until the rice is cooked to taste. Sprinkle with the remaining 2 tablespoons sesame seeds and the remaining tablespoon parsley.

Monkfish and Almond Paella, Alicante Style

(Arroz con Rape y Almendras al Estilo de Alicante)

Monkfish, sometimes called poor man's lobster, need not be compared to lobster, for it is a great fish in its own right. It does, however, have a texture and taste somewhat like lobster and is always excellent in paella because it does not flake and fall apart.

This distinctive paella is in the style of Alicante with an emphasis on the broth, which is made with some tomato, dried red pepper (substituted by fresh peppers and paprika in this recipe), and lots of garlic. The ingredients are few and simple, and most of the flavor is, in fact, in the broth, although the almonds also make their contribution to the taste of the rice and, when sautéed and sprinkled over the finished rice, add a certain crunchiness and rich flavor as well.

Serves 6

8 cups clam juice or Fish Broth
   (page 208)
1 medium onion, peeled
9 tablespoons olive oil
¾ cup slivered blanched almonds
   (about 3½ ounces)
2 heads garlic, separated into
   cloves and skin removed
2 medium red bell peppers,
   coarsely chopped
1 medium tomato, coarsely
   chopped

7 tablespoons minced parsley
¼ teaspoon crumbled thread
   saffron
2 tablespoons sweet paprika,
   preferably Spanish smoked
1¼ pounds monkfish or other
   firm-fleshed fish steaks,
   such as grouper, skin removed
   and cut in ¾-inch cubes
Kosher or sea salt
3 cups imported Spanish or
   Arborio short-grain rice

Combine the clam juice and onion in a large pot. Heat 3 tablespoons of the oil in a paella pan measuring 17–18 inches at its widest point (or in a shallow casserole of a similar size), over 2 burners if necessary. Sauté the almonds over medium-high heat until lightly browned. Remove with a slotted spoon and drain on paper towels. Transfer 6 tablespoons of the almonds to a mortar or miniprocessor and reserve the remaining 6 tablespoons separately. Sauté the garlic cloves until lightly browned, then transfer 2 garlic cloves to the mortar and leave the rest in the pan. Add the red peppers and sauté another 2 minutes. Add the tomato and 2 tablespoons of the parsley, and continue to cook another 2 minutes. Turn off the heat.

Stir in the saffron and paprika, and transfer the pan mixture to the pot. Take a few table-spoons of liquid from the pot and add to the paella pan to loosen whatever remains in the pan, then return to the pot. Bring the pot to a boil and simmer, uncovered, 20 minutes. Wipe out the paella pan. Meanwhile, mash the almonds and garlic in the mortar, along with 2 tablespoons of the parsley and ⅛ teaspoon salt. Add 4 teaspoons of the broth and mash as finely as possible.

Preheat the oven to 400° F for gas oven, 450° F for electric.

Strain the broth, pushing through as much of the solid matter as possible. Return 6 cups to the pot and keep hot over the lowest heat.

Sprinkle the fish all over with salt. Heat the remaining 6 tablespoons oil in the paella pan. Sauté the fish over high heat for 1 minute or so (it should not be fully cooked) and remove to a platter. Add the rice and sauté 1–2 minutes, until the rice is well coated with the oil. Pour in the hot broth and bring to a boil. Taste for salt and continue to boil about 3 minutes, stirring and rotating the pan occasionally. Stir in the monkfish, any juices from the platter, and the mortar mixture, and continue boiling about 2 minutes more, until the rice is no longer soupy but suffi-cient liquid remains to continue cooking the rice.

Transfer to the oven and cook, uncovered, 10–12 minutes in a gas oven, 15–20 minutes electric, until the rice is almost al dente. Remove to a warm spot, cover with foil, and let sit 5–10 minutes, until the rice is cooked to taste. Sprinkle with the reserved almonds and the remaining 3 tablespoons parsley.

Salmon and Asparagus Paella with Capers and Dill

(Paella de Salmón y Espárragos con Alcaparras y Eneldo)

Here is a paella that uses many ingredients that are traditional accompaniments to salmon. Since salmon is a strong-flavored fish, it can overpower the rice, and that's why I like to bridge the gap with a sprinkling of onion, capers, dill, egg, and smoked salmon over the cooked rice. Don't think of this topping as a mere garnish—its flavor is important to the success of this paella.

Serves 6

TOPPING

3 tablespoons minced onion

3 tablespoons whole nonpareil or larger capers, chopped

1 pound boneless fresh salmon, skin removed and cut in ½-inch cubes

Kosher or sea salt

½ cup dry white wine

5½ cups clam juice or Fish Broth (page 208)

¼ teaspoon crumbled thread saffron

8 tablespoons olive oil

1 medium onion, finely chopped

1 medium green bell pepper, finely chopped

4 cloves garlic, minced

1 large scallion, finely chopped

1½ tablespoons minced fresh dill

2 hard-boiled eggs, finely chopped

6 ounces chopped smoked salmon

4 tablespoons fresh chives, chopped, or freeze-dried

2 tablespoons fresh dill, chopped, or 1 teaspoon dried

1 medium tomato, finely chopped

½ teaspoon paprika, preferably Spanish smoked

2 teaspoons whole nonpareil or larger capers, chopped

3 cups imported Spanish or Arborio short-grain rice

12 cooked green asparagus spears

Put each of the topping ingredients into a small serving bowl or mix them together in one bowl. Sprinkle the salmon cubes with salt and let sit 10 minutes at room temperature. Combine in a pot the wine, clam juice, and saffron. Keep hot over the lowest heat. Preheat the oven to 400° F for gas oven, 450° F for electric.

Heat the oil in a paella pan measuring 17–18 inches at its widest point (or in a shallow casserole of a similar size), over 2 burners if necessary, and sauté the salmon over high heat until lightly browned (it should not be fully cooked). Remove to a warm platter. Lower the heat to medium and sauté the onion, green pepper, garlic, scallion, chives, and dill until the onions and pepper are softened. Turn up the heat, add the tomato, and cook 2 minutes, then stir in the paprika and capers. Add the rice and coat well with the pan mixture. Pour in all the hot broth, bring to a boil, and boil 2 minutes. Add the reserved salmon and continue to boil until the rice is no longer soupy but sufficient liquid remains to continue cooking the rice, about 3 minutes.

Arrange the asparagus attractively on top of the rice and place in the oven for 10–12 minutes in a gas oven, 15–20 minutes electric, until the liquid is absorbed and the rice is almost al dente. Remove to a warm spot, cover with foil, and let sit 5–10 minutes, until the rice is cooked to taste. Serve, passing the toppings separately.

SALT COD PAELLAS

For millennia salt cod has been considered survival food because of its ability to be stored for months at a time without refrigeration. In fact, the trade in cod-fish is often credited with being the reason for the spread of civilization. Cod may look somewhat unappetizing in its dried state, but when it is desalted, it becomes—especially in Spanish cooking—food for the gods. (Guría, one of the most celebrated restaurants in Spain's Basque Country, bases its fine reputation on its heavenly cod dishes.)

There seem to be more traditional recipes for paella using salt cod than for paella with any other ingredient. Perhaps it is because of cod's long association with Lent and the fact that cod combines exceptionally well with rice to make a hearty meatless meal. Curiously, cod is often not desalted for paella, in which case a broth without salt is used to cook the rice. And cod is always used sparingly in paella so that its taste will not be overwhelming.

Dried cod has certainly fallen out of favor in America; nevertheless, during the Christmas and Easter holidays, when it is traditional fare for many ethnic groups, it is easy enough to find at neighborhood Italian and Greek delicatessens. Look for cod that is well dried and almost white.

Cod, Beans, and Hot Green Pepper Paella

(Paella de Bacalao, Habichuelas, y Pimientos Picantes)

Start the preparation several days in advance.

Exceptional—and made even more delicious by the added jolt of a garlic sauce (ajo aceite) *of olive oil, garlic, and hot peppers drizzled over the finished rice. The salt cod is not over- powering (you may not even notice it is there), but unquestionably it gives a wonderfully complex flavor. You could substitute fresh monkfish; it will make a good rice but will cer- tainly not be the same dish.*

Serves 6 to 8

¼ pound dried boneless salt cod
  or ¾ pound fresh monkfish,
  about 1 inch thick (if the cod
  is thicker, slice in half
  lengthwise)
Garlic Sauce (*ajo aceite*) (page 209)
1 cup canned kidney beans
3½ cups clam juice, diluted with
  ½ cup water, or Fish Broth
  (page 208)
¼ teaspoon crumbled thread
  saffron
8 tablespoons olive oil

4 elongated, mildly hot green
  peppers, cored, seeded, and
  finely chopped
1 medium green bell pepper, finely
  chopped
6 cloves garlic, minced
2 medium tomatoes, skinned,
  seeded, and chopped
½ teaspoon sweet paprika,
  preferably Spanish smoked
3 cups imported Spanish or
  Arborio short-grain rice
Kosher or sea salt

Soak the cod in cold water to cover in the refrigerator for 2–3 days, changing the water once or twice daily until desalted to taste. Drain and dry between paper towels and chop very coarsely, then set aside.

Make the garlic sauce according to the instructions and transfer to a serving bowl.

Drain the beans over a bowl and add about 1½ cups water (you need exactly 2 cups of liquid). Transfer to a pot and add the diluted clam juice and saffron. Keep the broth hot over the lowest heat.

Preheat the oven to 400° F for gas oven, 450° F for electric.

Heat the oil in a paella pan measuring 17–18 inches at its widest point (or in a shallow casserole of a similar size), over 2 burners if necessary. Sauté the cod over medium heat, about 1 minute to each side. Remove to a warm platter. Add the hot and sweet peppers to the pan and sauté, stirring occasionally, until the peppers are slightly softened. Add the garlic and cook 1 minute. Add the tomatoes and the reserved cod, and cook 2 minutes more. Stir in the paprika, add the rice, and coat well with the pan mixture.

Pour in the hot broth and bring to a boil. Taste for salt, add the beans, and continue to boil, stirring and rotating the pan occasionally, until the rice is no longer soupy but sufficient liquid remains to continue cooking the rice, about 5 minutes.

Transfer to the oven and cook, uncovered, until the rice is almost al dente, 10–12 minutes in a gas oven, 15–20 minutes electric. Remove to a warm spot, cover with foil, and let sit 5–10 minutes, until the rice is cooked to taste. Serve, passing the garlic sauce separately.

Cod, Cauliflower, and Artichoke Paella

(Arroz con Bacalao, Coliflor, y Alcachofas)

The dried cod in this paella is hardly desalted, but don't worry. The cod's saltiness is tempered by eliminating salt in cooking and by using mostly water, rather than broth, for the cooking liquid. Every time you bite into a nugget of cod, its zesty flavor is a pleasant surprise—and a real contribution to the success of this rice. Cauliflower and artichokes are the perfect counterpoints.

Serves 4 to 6

½ pound dried boneless salt cod

6 cloves garlic, minced

¼ teaspoon crumbled thread saffron

2 cloves

2 tablespoons minced parsley

1 cup clam juice or Fish Broth (page 208)

4 cups water

8 tablespoons olive oil

2 medium onions, finely chopped

4 medium green frying peppers ("Italian") or 2 green bell peppers, finely chopped

1 medium tomato, finely chopped

4 frozen artichoke hearts, quartered

¾ pound cauliflower (about 6 flowers), cut into ½- to 1-inch florettes, stems removed

½ teaspoon paprika, preferably Spanish smoked

Freshly ground pepper

¼ cup frozen or fresh peas

2½ cups imported Spanish or Arborio short-grain rice

Salt

1 pimiento, cut in ½-inch strips for garnish

Rinse all of the salt from the cod and dry on paper towels. In a mortar or miniprocessor, mash as fine as possible the garlic, saffron, cloves, and parsley. Add 1 teaspoon water and continue mashing to a paste.

Combine the clam juice and 4 cups water in a saucepan and keep hot over the lowest heat.

Preheat the oven to 400° F for gas oven, 450° F for electric. Heat the oil in a paella pan measuring 17–18 inches at its widest point (or in a shallow casserole of a similar size), placing over

2 burners if necessary. Sauté the cod over medium-high heat, about 1 minute to each side, until slightly softened. Remove to a platter, leaving the oil in the pan.

Cut the cod in ½-inch strips and soak in warm water for about 30 minutes, changing the water several times. Drain and dry on paper towels, pressing to extract the salt and moisture. Shred.

Reheat the oil and sauté the onions and peppers over medium-high heat until slightly softened. Add the tomato, artichokes, and cauliflower, and continue cooking 3 minutes more. Stir in the paprika, pepper to taste, peas, rice, and the reserved cod, coating the rice well with the pan mixture. Pour in the hot broth and bring to a boil. Add the mortar mixture and salt to taste, and continue to boil, stirring and rotating the pan, until the rice is no longer soupy but sufficient liquid remains to continue cooking the rice, about 5 minutes.

Garnish with the pimiento, transfer to the oven, and cook, uncovered, until the rice is almost al dente, 10–12 minutes in a gas oven, 15–20 minutes electric. Remove to a warm spot, cover with foil, and let sit 5–10 minutes, until the rice is cooked to taste.

Cod Paella, Catalan Style

(Paella de Bacalao a la Catalana)

Start the preparation several days in advance.

Spinach sautéed with raisins and pine nuts is a well-known Catalan dish of exquisite taste that dates back to medieval times. In Catalan cooking, dried cod is prepared with these same ingredients, and although the blend of flavors may seem unlikely, it works wonderfully well. With the addition of rice the result is a succulent paella with just a hint of sweetness. If you eliminate the cod, this paella becomes a great vegetarian dish.

Serves 6

½ pound boneless salt cod, about ¾ inch thick (if thicker, slice to this thickness)

4 tablespoons raisins

6 cups clam juice or Fish Broth (page 208)

¼ teaspoon crumbled thread saffron

8 tablespoons olive oil

4 tablespoons pine nuts

2 medium onions, finely chopped

½ green bell pepper, finely chopped

1 small to medium tomato, finely chopped

10 cloves garlic, minced

4 tablespoons minced parsley

¾ pound spinach, thick stems trimmed, well washed, dried, and chopped (about 6 cups)

¾ cup dry white wine

3 cups Spanish or Arborio short-grain rice

Soak the cod in cold water to cover in the refrigerator for 2–3 days, changing the water once or twice daily, until desalted to taste. Drain and dry on paper towels.

Soak the raisins in warm water for 15 minutes, then drain.

Combine the clam juice and saffron in a saucepan and keep hot over the lowest heat.

Preheat the oven to 400° F for a gas oven, 450° F for electric.

Heat the oil in a paella pan measuring 17–18 inches, over 2 burners if necessary, and sauté the cod over medium heat about 1 minute on each side. Shred with your fingers or finely chop and reserve. Sauté the pine nuts until lightly brown, then add the onions and green pepper, and sauté until slightly softened. Stir in the tomato, garlic, and parsley, and cook 1–2 minutes, then add the spinach and sauté until wilted. Pour in the wine and cook away.

Add the rice and coat well with the pan mixture. Pour in the hot clam juice, add the reserved raisins and cod, and bring to a boil. Taste for salt and continue boiling, stirring and rotating the pan occasionally, until the rice is no longer soupy but sufficient liquid remains to continue cooking the rice, about 5 minutes.

Transfer to the oven and cook, uncovered, 10–12 minutes in a gas oven, 15–20 minutes electric, until the rice is almost al dente. Remove to a warm spot, cover with foil, and let sit 5–10 minutes, until the rice is cooked to taste.

Meat, Poultry, and Game Paellas

Ruperto's Marinated Chicken Paella

Sweet-and-Sour Chicken Paella with
Honey-Coated Walnuts

Crusted Paella with Pork, Chicken, and Sausage

Chicken Paella, Andalusian Style

Chicken, Peppers, and Eggplant "Samfaina" Paella

Chicken Pepitoria Paella

Valencia's Traditional Paella

Rabbit Paella with Red Pepper and Almonds

Stewed Rabbit Paella

Duck Paella, Sevilla Style

Tropical Paella "Tasca del Puerto"

Quail and Mushroom Paella

Cumin-Scented Pork and Watercress Paella

Marinated Pork Chop Paella

Pork and Pomegranate Paella

Rice with Pork, Potato, and Baked Eggs, Galician Style

Pork, Chickpea, and Red Pepper Paella

Catalan-Style Paella

Chorizo and Olive Paella "Santa Clara"

Mushroom and Meatball Paella, La Dársena Style

Tino's Chickpea Stew Paella

Cabbage and Chopped Meat Paella

Lamb and Red Pepper Paella

Lamb, Lentil, and Eggplant Paella

Rabbit, Spinach and Artichoke Paella

PORK PRODUCTS:
INDISPENSABLE INGREDIENTS
OF THE SPANISH LARDER

Pork has played a major culinary and historic role in Spain since Roman times, when Spanish hams were prized throughout the Empire. In the Middle Ages pork became a measure of religious belief. After centuries of Moorish domination and Jewish influence over Spain, the Catholic kings Fernando and Isabel, anxious for national unity, expelled those of other faiths or required them to convert. Eating pork—prohibited by both Arabs and Jews—was now the mark of a good Christian (not incidentally, pork was also ideal food for a poor country, since virtually nothing went to waste). One of Spain's most traditional dishes, *cocido* (chickpea stew) was originally a Sephardic preparation called *adafina* (its very slow cooking did not require human intervention during the Sabbath), but its Christian adaptation incorporated a wide range of pork products.

In fact, among the secrets of the remarkably robust flavors of so many Spanish dishes—even fish dishes—is the presence of pork, and in particular of cured ham *(jamón)*. Although Valencia is not generally known as a ham producer (fine air-dried ham requires a cooler, drier climate), the Aragonese province of Teruel that adjoins the Valencia region is famous for its hams, and Valencia has other wonderful pork products, like *longaniza* and the typically Valencian cooked black and white sausages.

In *Paella!* you will find first course and tapas dishes that combine diced ham with mushrooms, with shrimp and scallops. Ham is an ingredient in Shrimp and Fish Balls and a delightful flavor accent to Baked Vegetable Medley with Toasted Garlic. Cured ham appears repeatedly in paella recipes; it is present in Scallop and Mushroom Paella, in several chicken paellas and pork paellas, in Bean-Pebbled Paella, and in Potpourri of Mushrooms Paella.

One extraordinary kind of ham—Iberian ham from the native Iberian pig that grazes on a steady diet of acorns—has become a food cult in Spain and is eaten with abandon, despite its sometimes astonishing price. It is a highlight of my visits to Spain. Hams typically hang by the dozens from the rafters of Spanish bars and taverns, and when cut into thin slices *jamón* is indeed an exquisite appetite teaser. Alas, Iberian ham is not yet available in America, but Spanish serrano ham, another high quality product with fine flavor, is now imported on a limited basis and already has an ardent following.

Ruperto's Marinated Chicken Paella

(Paella de Pollo Adobado "Ruperto")

Ruperto's tapas bar is a legend in Sevilla, and his tapas keep bringing in the crowds. Although he does not serve paella at Casa Ruperto, he offered me his personal recipe, which uses the same marinade that makes his famous grilled quail and skewered pork so special. This is a succulent rice of exceptional flavor; the chicken, subtly seasoned with sherry, cumin, thyme, and nutmeg, and the marinade, which is incorporated into the paella's broth, bring a perfect balance to this dish.

Serves 6

One 3- to 3½-pound chicken

Marinade (page 178), increasing
   the recipe fourfold but only
   increasing the oil to 4 tablespoons

Kosher or sea salt

6 cups chicken broth, canned or
   homemade (page 207)

¼ teaspoon crumbled thread
   saffron

4 tablespoons olive oil

6 cloves garlic, minced

1 medium onion, finely chopped

2 medium green bell peppers,
   finely chopped

1 bay leaf

1 medium tomato, finely chopped

3 tablespoons minced parsley

3 cups imported Spanish or
   Arborio short-grain rice

¼ cup frozen peas

Cut the chicken wings in 2 parts, discarding the tips. Chop off the bony end of the legs. Divide the rest of the chicken into quarters, then cut with kitchen shears into 2-inch pieces.

Combine all the marinade ingredients in a large shallow bowl. Add the chicken, turning to coat well. Marinate at least 1 hour at room temperature.

Remove the chicken pieces from the marinade (reserving the marinade but discarding the garlic) and dry on paper towels. Sprinkle all over with salt.

In a large pot, combine the chicken broth with the remaining marinade (swirl a little of the chicken broth in the bowl to remove it all) and the saffron. Keep hot over the lowest heat.

Preheat the oven to 400° F for gas oven, 450° F for electric.

Heat the oil in a paella pan measuring 17–18 inches at its widest point (or in a shallow casserole of a similar size), over 2 burners if necessary. Sauté the chicken over high heat, turning once, about 5 minutes (it should not be fully cooked). Remove to a warm platter. Add to the pan the garlic, onion, green peppers, and bay leaf, and sauté until the vegetables are slightly softened. Stir in the tomato and parsley, and cook another 1–2 minutes.

Add the rice and coat well with the pan mixture. Pour in all the hot broth and bring to a boil. Add the peas, taste for salt, and continue boiling, stirring and rotating the pan occasionally, until the rice is no longer soupy but sufficient liquid remains to continue cooking the rice, about 5 minutes.

Discard the bay leaf and arrange the chicken pieces over the rice. Transfer to the oven and cook, uncovered, until the rice is almost al dente, 10–12 minutes in a gas oven, 15–20 minutes electric. Remove to a warm spot, cover with foil, and let sit 5–10 minutes, until the rice is cooked to taste.

Sweet-and-Sour Chicken Paella with Honey-Coated Walnuts

(Paella de Pollo Agridulce con Nueces Garapiñadas)

Honey-coated walnuts are essential to balance the sweet-and-sour character of this paella. The paella's oranges (Valencia's other major contribution to world gastronomy) are altogether traditional, but the sweetened walnuts and the blend of sweet and sour were suggested to me by old Spanish recipes of Moorish origin. The result is a unique paella that could not have a more fascinating range of tastes and textures.

For exceptionally crisp candied walnuts, make them as for caramelized pine nuts, page 198.

Serves 6 to 8

One 3- to 3½-pound chicken
Kosher or sea salt
2 tablespoons sugar
5⅓ cups plus 1 tablespoon Chicken Broth (page 207) or canned
⅔ cup plus 1 tablespoon orange juice, preferably freshly squeezed
2 tablespoons semisweet (*oloroso*) sherry or wine
2 teaspoons wine vinegar
5 tablespoons honey
¾ cup chopped walnuts, about ½ inch in size

¼ teaspoon crumbled thread saffron
8 tablespoons olive oil
1 medium onion, finely chopped
6 cloves garlic, minced
2 medium red bell peppers, finely chopped
2 medium tomatoes, finely chopped
4 tablespoons minced parsley
3 cups imported Spanish or Arborio short-grain rice
¼ pound snap peas or snow peas, strings removed
Orange slices, rind on, and cut in half, for garnish

Cut the chicken wings in 2 parts, discarding the tips. Chop off the bony end of the legs. Divide the rest of the chicken into quarters. Then cut with kitchen shears into 2-inch pieces. Sprinkle the chicken all over with salt.

In a small saucepan, heat the sugar and 2 tablespoons water over medium heat, stirring frequently, until the sugar is lightly caramelized. Slowly and carefully pour in 1 tablespoon of the chicken broth, 1 tablespoon of the orange juice, the sherry, vinegar, and 1 tablespoon of the honey. Stir and set aside.

In a small skillet, combine the remaining 4 tablespoons honey with the walnuts. Cook over low heat until the honey thickens and clings to the walnuts, about 8 minutes. Cool on greased foil.

Combine the remaining 5⅓ cups broth and ⅔ cup orange juice with the saffron in a pot and keep hot over the lowest heat.

Preheat the oven to 400° F for gas oven, 450° F for electric.

Heat the oil in a paella pan measuring 17–18 inches at its widest point (or in a shallow casserole of a similar size), over 2 burners if necessary. Sauté the chicken over high heat, about 5 minutes, turning once, until brown (it should not be fully cooked). Remove to a warm platter, leaving the oil in the pan.

Spoon a little of the reserved sweet-and-sour mixture over the chicken pieces. Combine the rest with the chicken broth mixture.

In the paella pan, sauté the onion, garlic, and red peppers over medium-high heat until the peppers are slightly softened. Add the tomatoes and parsley, and cook 2 minutes more, then stir in the rice and coat well with the pan mixture. Pour in the hot broth and bring to a boil. Taste for salt and continue to boil, stirring and rotating the pan occasionally if over 2 burners, until the rice is no longer soupy but sufficient liquid remains to continue cooking the rice about 5 minutes.

Mix in the snap peas, arrange the chicken pieces over the rice, and transfer to the oven. Cook, uncovered, until the rice is almost al dente, 10–12 minutes in a gas oven, 15–20 minutes electric. Remove to a warm spot, cover with foil, and let sit 5–10 minutes, until the rice is cooked to taste. Garnish with the orange slices and serve, sprinkling each portion with the honey-coated walnuts.

Crusted Paella with Pork, Chicken, and Sausage

(Arroz con Costra)

A deliciously flavored rice of pork, chicken, and sausage with an interesting twist: a tasty egg crust that allows the rice to be cut like a deep-dish pizza. This age-old recipe is similar to one found in the classic Llibre del Cuiner, *a sixteenth-century cookbook written by Ruperto de Nola, Catalan chef to the Spanish king of Naples. (Naples was at the time a part of Spain's empire.)*

I prefer to use chicken thigh meat for this recipe because it is the most succulent, and I find bratwurst sausage (somewhat like Catalan butifarra *sausage) properly firm and low in fat.*

Because of the egg coating and the fact that the rice can be "sliced," this paella is great for brunch.

Serves 4

⅔ cup canned chickpeas (reserve the liquid)

About 3 cups Chicken Broth (page 207) or canned

⅛ teaspoon crumbled thread saffron

¼ pound boneless chicken, preferably thigh meat, cut in ½-inch cubes

¼ pound lean boneless pork loin, cut in ½-inch cubes

Kosher or sea salt

Freshly ground pepper

4 tablespoons olive oil

¼ pound sausage, preferably bratwurst, cut on the diagonal in ½-inch slices

1 small onion, finely chopped

1 large clove garlic, minced

½ red bell pepper

1 small to medium tomato, finely chopped

1 tablespoon minced parsley

¼ teaspoon sweet paprika, preferably Spanish smoked

1¾ cups Spanish or Arborio short-grain rice

4 eggs

Drain the chickpeas and combine the liquid with the chicken broth and saffron to make 3½ cups. Mash half of the chickpeas through a strainer into the broth mixture. Keep the broth hot over the lowest heat.

Preheat the oven to 400° F for gas oven, 450° F for electric.

Sprinkle the chicken and pork all over with salt and pepper. Heat the oil in a paella pan that measures about 13 inches at its widest point (or in a casserole of a similar size). Sauté the chicken, pork, and sausage until lightly browned (they should not be fully cooked). Remove to a warm platter. Add the onion, garlic, and red pepper, and sauté until slightly softened. Add the tomato and parsley, and cook 2 minutes more. Stir in the paprika, then add the rice and coat well with the pan mixture.

Add the hot broth to the pan and bring to a boil. Taste for salt and stir in the remaining half of the chickpeas and the reserved chicken and pork (the sausage will be added later). Continue to boil, stirring occasionally, until the rice is no longer soupy but sufficient liquid remains to continue cooking the rice, about 5 minutes.

Transfer to the oven for 10–12 minutes in a gas oven, 15–20 minutes electric, until the rice is almost al dente. Remove from the oven.

Raise the oven temperature to 550° F. In a small bowl, beat the eggs well with a fork, adding a little salt. Pour the egg over the rice and garnish with the sausage. Return to the oven for about 10 minutes, until the egg coating is golden brown. Remove to a warm spot and let sit, uncovered, for 5 minutes. To serve, cut in wedges and transfer to individual plates using a metal spatula.

Chicken Paella, Andalusian Style

(Arroz con Pollo Estilo Andaluz)

Although basically a chicken paella, this rice adds several elements that make it special: a mash of sautéed almonds and garlic, Andalusian dry sherry, and a variety of vegetables that includes mushrooms, green beans, peppers, and asparagus.

Serves 6

7 tablespoons olive oil

2 tablespoons slivered blanched almonds

4 cloves garlic, minced

2 tablespoons minced parsley

¼ teaspoon crumbled thread saffron

¼ cup dry (*fino*) sherry or dry white wine

One 3- to 3½-pound chicken

Kosher or sea salt

5 cups chicken broth, canned or homemade (page 207)

1 medium onion, finely chopped

1 cup finely chopped green bell pepper

1 bay leaf

¼ cup diced Spanish serrano ham or prosciutto, cut from a ⅛-inch-thick slice

2 medium tomatoes, skinned, seeded, and finely chopped

1½ cups coarsely chopped oyster or other mild-flavored mushrooms, brushed clean and with thick stems trimmed

¼ pound cooked green beans, cut in 1-inch lengths

2½ cups imported Spanish or Arborio short-grain rice

16 cooked asparagus spears

1 pimiento, cut in ½-inch strips

In a small skillet, heat 1 tablespoon of the oil and sauté the almonds and garlic until golden. Transfer to a mortar or miniprocessor, add the parsley and saffron, and mash to a paste. Stir in the sherry.

Cut the chicken wings in 2 parts, discarding the tips. Chop off the bony end of the legs. Divide the rest of the chicken into quarters, then cut with kitchen shears into 2-inch pieces. Sprinkle all over with salt.

Pour the broth into a pot and keep warm over the lowest heat.

Preheat the oven to 400° F for gas oven, 450° F for electric.

Heat the remaining 6 tablespoons oil in a paella pan measuring 17–18 inches at its widest point (or in a shallow casserole of a similar size), over 2 burners if necessary. Sauté the chicken over high heat for 5 minutes, turning once. Remove to a warm platter. Reduce the heat and add to the pan the onion, green pepper, bay leaf, and ham, and sauté until the onion and pepper are slightly softened. Add the tomatoes, mushrooms, and green beans, and sauté 5 minutes more.

Stir in the rice, coating well with the pan mixture. Pour in the hot broth and bring to a boil. Add the mortar mixture, taste for salt, and continue to boil, stirring and rotating the pan occasionally, until the rice is no longer soupy but sufficient liquid remains to continue cooking the rice, about 5 minutes. Discard the bay leaf. Add the chicken pieces and any juices from the platter.

Arrange the asparagus and pimiento strips attractively over the rice and transfer to the oven. Cook, uncovered, until the rice is almost al dente, 10–15 minutes in a gas oven, 15–20 minutes electric. Remove to a warm spot, cover with foil, and let sit 5–10 minutes, until the rice is cooked to taste.

Chicken, Peppers, and Eggplant "Samfaina" Paella

(Arroz de Pollo y Samfaina)

The sweetness given by the substantial amount of peppers and onions in this paella is balanced by the contrasting taste of roasted eggplant—both in the rice and for garnishing the paella (in this case the garnish is also an important textural element). Samfaina is a Catalan term for a slow-cooked blend, or "symphony," of onion, peppers, tomatoes, and eggplant—vegetables that may also join forces with chicken to create a delicious stew.

The chicken in this paella appears both over the rice and in small pieces mixed into the rice for additional flavor.

Serves 4

Two ½-pound eggplants, cut crosswise into twenty ¼-inch rounds, the rest partially skinned with a potato peeler and cut in ½-inch cubes

Kosher or sea salt

4 cloves garlic, minced

1 tablespoon minced parsley

Half of a 3-pound chicken

6 tablespoons olive oil

Freshly ground pepper

3 cups Chicken Broth (page 207) or canned

⅛ teaspoon crumbled thread saffron

2 tablespoons diced Spanish serrano ham or prosciutto, cut from a ¼-inch-thick slice

1 large onion, preferably Spanish or Vidalia, slivered

1 medium green bell pepper, cut in ½-inch strips

1 medium red bell pepper, cut in ½-inch strips

1½ teaspoons thyme leaves or ¼ teaspoon dried

1 bay leaf

1 large tomato, finely chopped

½ cup dry white wine

3 cups imported Spanish or Arborio short-grain rice

Arrange the eggplant slices and cubes in a colander and sprinkle well with salt, mixing to distribute the salt. Leave for 20 minutes to drain. Meanwhile, mash to a paste in a mortar or miniprocessor the garlic, parsley, and ⅛ teaspoon salt.

Cut the chicken thigh into 1½- to 2-inch pieces with a knife or with kitchen shears. Cut off the bony end of the leg and divide the wings in 2 pieces, discarding the tip. Cut the breast into ½-inch boneless cubes. Sprinkle the chicken all over with salt.

Preheat the oven to 425° F for gas oven, 475° F for electric.

Dry the eggplant on paper towels and transfer to a greased baking tray. Drizzle with 2 tablespoons olive oil, sprinkle with pepper, and bake in the oven for about 10 minutes, until tender. Leave the oven at this temperature for the paella.

Combine the broth and saffron in a pot and keep hot over the lowest heat. Heat the remaining 4 tablespoons oil in a paella pan measuring about 13 inches at its widest point (or in a shallow casserole of a similar size). Sauté all the chicken pieces except the breast cubes over high heat for about 5 minutes, turning once (they should not be fully cooked). Remove to a warm platter. Add the chicken breast cubes, sauté 1 minute, and remove. Add to the pan the ham, onion, green and red peppers, thyme, and bay leaf, cover with foil or with a lid, and continue cooking at medium-low heat for 20 minutes more.

Stir in the tomato, raise the heat, and cook, uncovered, until any liquid has evaporated. Add ¼ cup of the wine and boil away, then stir in the remaining ¼ cup wine and boil away again. Stir in the eggplant cubes, lower the heat, and cook 2 minutes more. Discard the bay leaf, then stir in the rice and coat well with the pan mixture.

Pour in the hot broth and the mortar mixture, and bring to a boil. Taste for salt and continue boiling, stirring occasionally, until the rice is no longer soupy but sufficient liquid remains to continue cooking the rice, about 5 minutes. Stir in the cubed chicken and arrange the rest of the chicken pieces and the eggplant slices over the rice.

Transfer to the oven and cook, uncovered, until the rice is almost al dente, 10–15 minutes in a gas oven, 15–20 minutes electric. (If the rice still has liquid, place the pan on top of the stove over high heat without stirring until it has boiled away). Remove to a warm spot, cover with foil, and let sit 5–10 minutes, until the rice is cooked to taste.

Chicken Pepitoria Paella
(Paella de Pollo en Pepitoria)

An out-of-the ordinary paella, even though its main ingredient is simply chicken. Pepitoria is an age-old preparation for chicken and rabbit. A touch of Spanish sherry and nutmeg lends a very distinctive taste, as does the mash (picada) of almonds, garlic, and parsley. The topping of parsley and chopped egg (egg is also a traditional ingredient of pepitoria) gives a pretty appearance and adds essential flavor as well.

Serves 6

One 3- to 3½-pound chicken
Kosher or sea salt
2 tablespoons blanched slivered
    almonds
6 cloves garlic, minced
10 tablespoons minced
    parsley
¼ teaspoon crumbled thread
    saffron
6 cups chicken broth, canned or
    homemade (page 207)
8 tablespoons olive oil
1 medium onion, finely
    chopped

¼ cup diced Spanish serrano ham
    or prosciutto, cut from a
    ¼-inch-thick slice
1 red bell pepper, finely chopped
1 bay leaf
1 medium tomato, finely chopped
A generous grating of nutmeg
1 teaspoon sweet paprika,
    preferably Spanish smoked
¼ cup dry (*fino*) sherry or dry
    white wine
1½ cups imported Spanish or
    Arborio short-grain rice
2 hard-boiled eggs, chopped

Cut the chicken wings into 2 parts, discarding the tips. Chop off the bony end of the legs. Divide the rest of the chicken into quarters. Then cut with kitchen shears into 2-inch pieces. Sprinkle the chicken all over with salt. Pour the broth into a large pot.

Mash to a paste in a mortar or miniprocessor the almonds, garlic, 6 tablespoons of the parsley, and the saffron. Stir in 1 tablespoon of the broth, and once it has been incorporated, stir in 1 more tablespoon. Set aside.

Keep the broth hot over the lowest heat.

Preheat the oven to 400° F for gas oven, 450° F for electric.

Heat the oil in a paella pan measuring about 13 inches at its widest point (or in a shallow casserole of a similar size). Brown the chicken over high heat, turning once, for about 5 minutes (do not remove from the pan).

Lower the heat to medium-high, add the onion, ham, red pepper, and bay leaf, and sauté until the vegetables are slightly softened. Add the tomato, cook 1 minute more, then stir in the nutmeg, paprika, and sherry. Cook away the sherry over high heat. Add the rice and coat well with the pan mixture, then pour in all the hot broth and bring to a boil. Add the mortar mixture, taste for salt, and continue to boil until the rice is no longer soupy but sufficient liquid remains to continue cooking the rice, about 5 minutes.

Discard the bay leaf and transfer the rice to the oven. Cook, uncovered, until the rice is almost al dente, 10–12 minutes in a gas oven, 15–20 minutes electric. Remove to a warm spot, cover with foil, and let sit 5–10 minutes, until the rice is cooked to taste. Sprinkle with 2 tablespoons of the parsley and with half of the chopped eggs. Serve, sprinkling the remaining eggs and parsley over each portion.

Valencia's Traditional Paella

(Paella a la Valenciana)

Here is the paella that started it all, the paella once made for lunch over an open fire in the fields of Valencia by day laborers. You can see why: All the ingredients were at hand, and it is quick cooking and needs no kitchen facilities to prepare (for the mixed meat and seafood paella that often goes by the name Valenciana, see page 122).

I have made two modifications, however; I have added a small amount of chicken broth for extra flavor and have finished the paella in the oven, since a home-size stove burner, even if the pan is turned occasionally, is not large enough to cook the rice evenly. If you choose to use an outdoor grill, by all means do all the cooking over the flame (see page 12 for further instructions).

I have omitted the land snails that are typical in this paella since they are not easy to find. When they are unavailable in Valencia, sprigs of rosemary are substituted. I'm not sure what the connection is, but the rosemary does give the rice an enticing scent. If you choose to use only chicken or rabbit, instead of a combination of both, just double the amount.

For this paella to be authentic, it must have a socarrat—a thin layer of rice at the bottom of the pan that becomes brown and crusty and is considered the quintessence of the paella. It is scraped off after the rice is served and passed around so everyone can have a share of it.

Serves 6 to 8

2 cups chicken broth, canned or
  homemade (page 207)
6 sprigs rosemary or ½ teaspoon
  dried rosemary leaves
Kosher or sea salt
¼ teaspoon crumbled thread
  saffron
Half of a 2½- to 3-pound chicken
Half of a 2- to 2½-pound rabbit
8 tablespoons olive oil
2 medium green frying ("Italian")
  peppers or 1 green bell pepper,
  finely chopped
1 medium onion, finely chopped

8 cloves garlic, minced
½ pound green beans, preferably
  broad, flat beans, ends snapped
  off and cut in half crosswise
½ pound snap peas or snow peas,
  strings removed
4 frozen artichoke hearts, in
  quarters
2 medium tomatoes, finely chopped
2 tablespoons minced parsley
1 teaspoon paprika, preferably
  Spanish smoked
3 cups imported Spanish or
  Arborio short-grain rice

Heat the broth, rosemary, salt, saffron, and 4 cups water in a covered pot over the lowest heat for 20 minutes. Remove the rosemary.

Cut the chicken wings in 2 parts, discarding the tip. Chop off the bony end of the leg. Divide the rest of the chicken into quarters, then cut with kitchen shears into 2-inch pieces. Do the same with the rabbit. Sprinkle all over with salt. Put aside a few snap peas for garnish.

Keep the broth hot over the lowest heat. Preheat the oven to 400° F for gas oven, 450° F for electric.

Heat the oil in a paella pan measuring 17–18 inches at its widest point (or in a shallow casserole of a similar size), over 2 burners if necessary. Sauté the chicken and rabbit over high heat until brown (it should not be fully cooked), about 5 minutes, turning once. Add the green peppers, onion, and garlic, and cook until slightly softened, keeping the heat high. Stir in the green beans, snap peas, and artichokes, and cook on high for about 3 minutes. Add the tomatoes and parsley, cook 1 minute, then mix in the paprika.

Stir in the rice and coat well with the pan mixture. Pour in the hot broth and bring to a boil. Taste for salt and continue to boil about 5 minutes, stirring and rotating the pan occasionally, until the rice is no longer soupy but enough liquid remains to continue cooking the rice, about 5 minutes.

Arrange the reserved snap peas over the rice and transfer to the oven. Cook, uncovered, until the rice is almost al dente, 10–12 minutes in a gas oven, 15–20 minutes electric.

Remove to a warm spot, cover with foil, and let sit 5–10 minutes, until the rice is cooked to taste. Return the paella to the stove over high heat and cook, without stirring, until a crust of rice forms at the bottom of the pan (be careful not to burn it).

Rabbit Paella with Red Pepper and Almonds

(Paella de Conejo con Pimientos y Almendras)

This rabbit paella is given a touch of sweetness by the red pepper and a punch of flavor by the toasted almonds and garlic added right before the paella goes to the oven. This paella is typically made in a fireproof earthenware casserole (see Sources, page 215) instead of a paella pan (although a paella pan can also be used). The result is a slightly moist rice.

Serves 6

One 2½-pound rabbit or small
   chicken, skin and fat removed
2 tablespoons slivered blanched
   almonds
1¼ cups canned chickpeas,
   drained and rinsed (reserve
   the liquid)
About 5½ cups chicken broth,
   canned or homemade
   (page 207)
4 cloves garlic, minced

2 tablespoons minced parsley
¼ teaspoon crumbled thread
   saffron
Kosher or sea salt
8 tablespoons olive oil
1 medium onion, finely chopped
1 red pepper, diced
2 medium to large tomatoes,
   finely chopped
3 cups imported Spanish or
   Arborio short-grain rice

Cut the rabbit with kitchen shears into pieces approximately 2 inches in size, discarding the bony tips of the legs. Sprinkle all over with salt.

Toast the almonds on a cookie sheet in a 350° F oven until lightly brown, about 4 minutes. Combine the liquid from the chickpeas with the broth to make 6 cups. Mash ½ cup of the chickpeas through a strainer into the broth. Reserve the remaining ¾ cup chickpeas for the rice (if there is more, keep for some other use).

In a mortar or miniprocessor, mash to a paste the garlic, parsley, saffron, almonds, and ¼ teaspoon salt. Mash in 1 tablespoon of the broth.

Keep the broth hot over the lowest heat. Preheat the oven to 400° F for gas oven, 450° F for electric.

Heat the oil in a shallow casserole measuring about 15 inches (or in a 17–18-inch paella pan) and sauté the rabbit over high heat about 5 minutes (it should not be fully cooked). Remove to a warm platter. Add the onion and pepper to the pan and cook slowly until the vegetables are slightly softened. Add the tomatoes, turn up the heat, and sauté 2 minutes more.

Stir in the rice and coat well with the pan mixture. Pour in the broth and bring to a boil. Add the reserved chickpeas, rabbit, and mortar mixture, and taste for salt. Continue to boil about 5 minutes, until the rice is no longer soupy but sufficient liquid remains to continue cooking the rice, about 5 minutes.

Transfer to the oven and cook 10–12 minutes in a gas oven, 15–20 minutes electric, until the rice is almost al dente. Remove to a warm spot, cover with foil, and let sit 5–10 minutes, until the rice is cooked to taste.

RABBIT PAELLAS

Rabbit is an exceptionally lean and tasty white meat that is exceedingly popular in Spain, where it has long been part of traditional cooking. (Hispania, the Roman name for Spain, means "land of rabbits.") Not surprisingly, its accessibility in Spain has made it a part of many paellas, especially Valencia's original paella (page 82), which was made outdoors by workers in the fields.

Readily available in supermarkets and butcher shops (usually frozen), rabbit is well worth trying if you are not already a fan, as I am. It is as versatile as chicken but without the fat. Rabbit is never eaten with the skin, so if you choose to substitute chicken, I suggest removing the skin.

Stewed Rabbit Paella

(Paella de Conejo Estofado)

This is one of my favorites, and although paella is meant to be a quick-cooking dish, stewing the meat first unquestionably contributes to the deeper, richer flavor of this rice and to the tenderness of the meat. It takes longer to make, but otherwise the work is the same.

Serves 6 to 8

One 2½-pound rabbit or small
    chicken
Kosher or sea salt
8 tablespoons olive oil
2 medium onions, finely chopped
2 red bell peppers, finely
    chopped
20 cloves garlic, minced
2 tablespoons minced parsley
6 cups plus 4 tablespoons chicken
    broth, canned or homemade
    (page 207)
4 tablespoons dry white wine

Two 1-inch pieces dried red chile
    pepper, or to taste
1 tablespoon chopped rosemary
    leaves or ½ teaspoon dried
1 tablespoon thyme leaves or
    ½ teaspoon dried
½ teaspoon sweet paprika,
    preferably Spanish smoked
2 bay leaves
¼ teaspoon crumbled thread
    saffron
3 cups imported Spanish or
    Arborio short-grain rice

Cut the rabbit into 1½-inch pieces, discarding the bony tips of the legs. Sprinkle all over with salt.

Heat 2 tablespoons of the oil in a shallow casserole and brown the rabbit over high heat, turning once. Add half of the chopped onions and red peppers, the garlic, and parsley, and cook over medium-high heat until the vegetables are slightly softened. Stir in 4 tablespoons of the broth, the wine, chile pepper, rosemary, thyme, paprika, and bay leaves. Cover and simmer 40 minutes.

Discard the bay leaves and chile pepper. If there is still a significant amount of liquid in the casserole, boil until reduced and thickened. Combine the remaining 6 cups broth and the saffron in a pot and keep hot over the lowest heat.

Preheat the oven to 400° F for gas oven, 450° F for electric.

Heat the remaining 5 tablespoons oil in a paella pan measuring 17–18 inches at its widest point (or in a shallow casserole of a similar size), over 2 burners if necessary. Sauté the remaining chopped onion and bell pepper over medium-high heat until slightly softened. Stir in the rice and coat well with the pan mixture. Pour in the hot broth and boil for about 3 minutes, stirring and rotating the pan occasionally if over 2 burners. Stir in the stewed rabbit, deglazing the casserole in which the rabbit cooked with some of the broth and adding it to the paella pan. Continue to boil until the rice is no longer soupy but sufficient liquid remains to continue cooking the rice, about 2 minutes more.

Transfer to the oven and cook until the rice is almost al dente, 10–12 minutes in a gas oven, 15–20 minutes electric. Remove to a warm spot, cover with foil, and let sit 5–10 minutes, until the rice is cooked to taste.

Duck Paella, Sevilla Style

(Paella de Pato a la Sevillana)

Duck simmered in a sauce of green olives and sherry is a special dish of Sevilla. Here, similar ingredients are used to make a great-tasting paella.

Ducks in Spain are lean—not the fatty kind we have here—so to make this paella it is necessary to roast the duck first to eliminate the fat.

Serves 4 to 6

One 4½- to 5-pound duck

Kosher or sea salt

½ cup coarsely chopped green olives

¾ cup plus 2 tablespoons dry white wine

About 4¾ cups chicken broth, canned or homemade (page 207)

½ cup dry *fino* sherry

¼ teaspoon crumbled thread saffron

7 tablespoons olive oil

¼ cup finely chopped onion

2 cloves garlic, minced

1 cup finely chopped red bell pepper

¼ cup finely chopped carrot

2 tablespoons minced parsley

1 tablespoon thyme leaves or ½ teaspoon dried

½ cup finely chopped tomato

3 cups imported Spanish or Arborio short-grain rice

Preheat the oven to 375° F.

Prick the duck deeply all over with a fork, sprinkle inside and out with salt, and place in a roasting pan, with the neck, if possible. Roast for 1 hour, pour off the fat, and roast 45 minutes more.

Meanwhile, combine in a saucepan the olives and 6 tablespoons of the white wine, and boil 5 minutes. Drain.

Remove the duck from the roasting pan. Separate the legs, discard the neck and wings, split the duck in half and remove the backbone. Cut the rest into 2-inch pieces. Deglaze the roasting pan with the remaining ½ cup white wine. Pour into a pot, and add the broth, and sherry. Measure to 6 cups, and stir in the saffron. Keep hot over the lowest heat.

Raise the oven to 400° F for gas oven, 450° F for electric.

Heat the oil in a paella pan measuring 17–18 inches at its widest point (or in a shallow casserole of a similar size), over 2 burners if necessary. Sauté the onion, garlic, pepper, carrot, parsley, and thyme over medium heat until the vegetables are softened, about 10 minutes. Add the tomato and cook 2 minutes more, then stir in the rice, coating it well with the oil. Pour in the hot broth and bring to a boil. Taste for salt and continue to boil, stirring and rotating the pan occasionally, until the rice is no longer soupy but sufficient liquid remains to continue cooking the rice, about 5 minutes.

Arrange the duck pieces over the rice and transfer to the oven. Cook, uncovered, until the rice is almost al dente, 10–12 minutes in a gas oven, 15–20 minutes electric. Remove to a warm spot, cover with foil, and let sit 5–10 minutes, until the rice is cooked to taste.

Tropical Paella "Tasca del Puerto"
(Arroz Tropical "Tasca del Puerto")

Reme and Ximo Boix, owners and chefs of the fine Tasca del Puerto restaurant in the city of Castellón de la Plana, are the only paella experts I know who dare to be different. This unusual paella is a prime example. They have taken traditional paella ingredients and embellished them with grapes, raisins, walnuts, and sesame oil to create an exceptional rice.

Serves 6 to 8

One 4- to 4½-pound duck, trussed
Kosher or sea salt
About 5½ cups chicken broth, canned or homemade (page 207)
½ cup dry white wine
¼ teaspoon crumbled thread saffron
7 tablespoons olive oil
2 tablespoons pine nuts
2 tablespoons chopped walnuts
1 red bell pepper, finely chopped
1 green bell pepper, finely chopped
4 tablespoons raisins
¼ pound spinach leaves, washed, well dried, and finely chopped (about 1 cup)
2 tablespoons minced parsley

½ pound cauliflower, in small florets
¼ pound green beans, preferably broad green beans, cut in 1-inch lengths
4 cloves garlic, finely chopped
2 medium tomatoes, finely chopped
2 teaspoons sweet paprika, preferably Spanish smoked
3 cups imported Spanish or Arborio short-grain rice
4 teaspoons sesame oil
½ cup cooked white beans, drained and rinsed
24 red seedless grapes
24 green seedless grapes
Pimiento strips for garnish

Preheat the oven to 375° F.

Prick the duck all over with a fork. Sprinkle inside and out with salt. Place in a roasting pan (with the neck, if available) and roast for 1 hour. Pour off the fat and roast 45 minutes more. Discard the neck and wings, split the duck in half, and remove the backbone. Separate the legs and cut the rest into 2-inch pieces. Deglaze the pan with ½ cup of the broth. Combine with more broth to make 5½ cups. Pour into a pot and mix with the wine and saffron. Keep hot over the lowest heat. Raise the oven to 400° F for gas oven, 450° F for electric.

Heat the oil in a paella pan measuring 17–18 inches at its widest point (or in a shallow casserole of a similar size), over 2 burners if necessary. Quickly sauté the pine nuts and walnuts until the pine nuts just begin to color. Add the red and green peppers, raisins, spinach, parsley, cauliflower, and green beans, and cook 5 minutes over medium heat. Stir in the garlic and tomatoes, and cook 2 minutes more, then mix in the paprika.

Add the rice and sesame oil, and coat well with the pan mixture. Pour in all the hot broth and bring to a boil. Taste for salt, add the white beans and red and green grapes, and continue to boil, stirring and rotating the pan occasionally, until the rice is no longer soupy but sufficient liquid remains to continue cooking the rice, about 5 minutes.

Arrange the duck pieces and the pimiento over the rice, transfer to the oven, and cook, uncovered, until the rice is almost al dente, 10–12 minutes in a gas oven, 15–20 minutes electric. Remove to a warm spot, cover with foil, and let sit 5–10 minutes, until the rice is cooked to taste.

Quail and Mushroom Paella
(Paella de Codornices y Setas)

Spain is internationally renowned game country, and quail is a particular favorite, far more likely to be found on restaurant menus than chicken. It seems to be gaining in popularity here, too; I can always find it—albeit usually frozen—at my local butcher or Italian specialty shop.

This paella is exceptionally good in part because of the added zest given by a small amount of slab bacon and by a mortar mash of garlic and herbs, which is brushed over the quail.

Serves 6 to 8

8 quail, split in half
Kosher or sea salt
6 cups chicken broth, canned or
 homemade (page 207)
¼ teaspoon crumbled thread
 saffron
9 tablespoons olive oil
4 tablespoons diced slab bacon
2 medium red bell peppers, cut in
 ½-inch dice
2 medium green bell peppers, cut
 in ½-inch dice
1 medium onion, finely chopped
½ pound mushrooms, such as
 shiitake, brushed clean, stems

trimmed, and very coarsely
 chopped
1 medium tomato, finely
 chopped
One 2-inch piece of dried
 red chile pepper or
¼ teaspoon crushed red
 pepper
8 cloves garlic, minced
1½ teaspoons thyme leaves or
 ¼ teaspoon dried
2 tablespoons minced parsley
1 cup dry white wine
3 cups Spanish or Arborio
 short-grain rice

Sprinkle the quail all over with salt. Combine the broth and saffron in a pot and keep hot over the lowest heat.

Preheat the oven to 400° F for gas oven, 450° F for electric.

Heat 6 tablespoons of the oil in a paella pan measuring 17–18 inches at its widest point (or in a shallow casserole of a similar size), over 2 burners if necessary. Sauté the quail over high heat, turning once, until lightly browned (they should not be fully cooked). Remove to a warm platter.

Lower the heat to medium, add the bacon, and cook until it releases its fat. Add the red and green peppers, onion, and mushrooms, and sauté until slightly softened. Stir in the tomato and chile pepper, and continue cooking until the vegetables are almost tender.

Meanwhile, in a mortar or miniprocessor, mash to a paste the garlic, thyme, parsley, and ⅛ teaspoon salt. Stir in the remaining 3 tablespoons oil and brush the quail lightly with a small amount of the mixture and reserve the rest.

Stir the wine into the tomato mixture and boil away. Discard the chile pepper, add the rice, and coat well with the pan mixture. Pour in all the hot broth and bring to a boil. Stir in the remaining mortar mixture, taste for salt, and continue to boil, stirring and rotating the pan occasionally, until the rice is no longer soupy but sufficient liquid remains to continue cooking the rice, about 5 minutes.

Arrange the quail over the rice. Transfer to the oven and cook, uncovered, until the rice is almost al dente, 10–12 minutes in a gas oven, 15–20 minutes electric. Remove to a warm spot, cover with foil, and let sit 5–10 minutes, until the rice is cooked to taste.

Cumin-Scented Pork and Watercress Paella

(Arroz de Magra y Berros al Comino)

The union of watercress and cumin in this splendid paella makes it hard to resist. I find myself still eating it long after my hunger has been sated. It is inspired by a hearty soup of Spain's Canary Islands, a region where watercress is a common ingredient in soups, stews, and salads, although it is rarely used on the Spanish mainland. An added bonus of this paella is that it is very easy to prepare.

Serves 4

3 cups chicken broth, canned or
    homemade (page 207)
⅛ teaspoon crumbled thread
    saffron
¾ pound boneless pork loin, cut in
    ½-inch cubes
Kosher or sea salt
4 tablespoons olive oil
¾ cup finely chopped onion
4 cloves garlic, minced
½ medium green bell pepper, finely
    chopped
1 bunch (about ½ pound)

watercress, thick stems trimmed,
    and chopped (about 3 cups)
1 tablespoon minced parsley
½ teaspoon ground cumin
½ teaspoon sweet paprika,
    preferably Spanish smoked
1½ cups imported Spanish or
    Arborio short-grain rice
½ cup cooked white beans, drained
    and rinsed
¼–½ pound small cooked red
    potatoes, peeled and cut in
    quarters or eighths

Combine the broth and saffron in a pot and keep hot over the lowest heat.

Preheat the oven to 400° F for gas oven, 450° F for electric.

Sprinkle the pork cubes all over with salt. Heat the oil in a paella pan measuring 13 inches at its widest point (or in a shallow casserole of a similar size). Sauté the pork over high heat for 1–2 minutes (it should not be fully cooked) and remove to a warm platter. Add the onion, garlic, and pepper, and cook over medium-high heat until the vegetables are slightly softened. Add the watercress and parsley, cook 1 minute to wilt the watercress, then mix in the cumin and paprika.

Stir in the rice and coat well with the pan mixture. Pour in all the hot broth and bring to a boil.

Stir in the beans and pork, taste for salt, and continue boiling, stirring occasionally, until the rice is no longer soupy but sufficient liquid remains to continue cooking the rice, about 5 minutes.

Mix in the cooked potatoes and transfer to the oven. Cook, uncovered, until the rice is almost al dente, 10–12 minutes in a gas oven, 15–20 minutes electric. Remove to a warm spot, cover with foil, and let sit 5–10 minutes, until the rice is cooked to taste.

LAS FALLAS:
VALENCIA'S ORGY OF FIRE

The five-day fiesta of Las Fallas begins March 15 and brings Valencia—the third largest city in Spain—to a virtual halt. This unique festival takes a full year to prepare, consumes untold hours of painstaking labor, and involves huge expenditures. And it goes up in flames in the space of an hour.

Fallas are elaborate oversized tableaux several stories high that are made of papier-maché and set aflame on the last night of the fiesta. They represent the continuation of a custom that began centuries ago when carpenters burned their discarded wood scraps in huge bonfires on March 19, the day of the city's patron saint, San José, to celebrate winter's end.

The rivalry is intense as each neighborhood produces elaborate *fallas*, set up in the city's squares for the duration of the fiesta, in hopes that theirs will be the year's prizewinner. From the victorious tableau one small figure, called a *ninot*, is spared and put on display in the Fallas Museum. The tableaux are satirical, exuberantly decorated, often gaudy, grotesque, and in downright bad taste, which is all part of the fun. When my husband and I travel to Valencia to witness Las Fallas, we join the crowds of Valencians strolling from square to square to admire each *falla*, munching all the while on typical *bunyols*—airy fritters that are fried outdoors in vats of oil, sprinkled with sugar, and served in paper cones.

But at midnight on March 19 a torch is put to each and every *falla*, creating huge bonfires in the city's squares. The largest *falla* is reserved for the monumental Plaza del País Valencià, where the scene resembles New York's Times Square on New Year's Eve. To the accompaniment of fireworks, bomblike blasts, and rhythmic strings of firecrackers, the last of the *fallas* goes up in flames. When it is all over, the city looks as if it had come under enemy rocket fire. Gradually the air settles into a smoky haze; the festival of *las fallas* has come to a sudden and dramatic conclusion. But there is no time to waste; planning, preparation, and anticipation of Las Fallas for the coming year have already begun.

Marinated Pork Chop Paella

(Arroz con Costillas Adobadas)

Start the preparation one day in advance.

Marinating pork in olive oil, garlic, paprika, and herbs is an age-old method once used to preserve pork and today a popular way to season it. In this tasty paella the marinade not only flavors the pieces of pork but lends a unique flavor to the rice.

Serves 5 to 6

MARINADE

2 tablespoons olive oil

1 tablespoon dry white wine

1½ teaspoons paprika, preferably Spanish smoked

2 cloves garlic, crushed to a paste in a mortar or garlic press

1 bay leaf

1 teaspoon thyme leaves or ⅛ teaspoon dried

¼ teaspoon dried oregano

Salt

Freshly ground pepper

1 pound rib pork chops, 1 inch thick, trimmed of fat and hacked into 1½-inch pieces with a heavy knife or by a butcher

6 cloves garlic, peeled

¼ teaspoon crumbled thread saffron

2 tablespoons minced parsley

Kosher or sea salt

¼ cup dry white wine

4¾ cups chicken broth, canned or homemade (page 207)

5 tablespoons olive oil

2 large red bell peppers, finely chopped

1 medium tomato, skinned, seeded, and finely chopped

2 teaspoons sweet paprika, preferably Spanish smoked

2½ cups imported Spanish or Arborio short-grain rice

⅔ cup frozen or fresh peas

Combine all marinade ingredients in a large bowl. Add the pork and stir to coat well. Cover and refrigerate overnight.

Mash to a paste in a mortar or miniprocessor the garlic, saffron, parsley, and ¼ teaspoon salt.

Stir in the wine. Keep the broth hot over the lowest heat. Remove the pork from the marinade and pat dry with paper towels. Add the remaining marinade to the broth.

Preheat the oven to 400° F for gas oven, 450° F for electric.

Heat the oil in a paella pan measuring 17–18 inches at its widest point (or in a shallow casserole of a similar size), over 2 burners if necessary. Sauté the pork until lightly browned over medium-high heat (it should not be fully cooked). Remove to a warm platter. Add the red peppers and sauté until slightly softened.

Add the tomato to the pan, cook 1–2 minutes, then stir in the paprika. Add the rice and stir to coat well with the pan mixture. Pour in all the hot broth and bring to a boil. Taste for salt, add the peas, and boil about 5 minutes more, until the rice is no longer soupy but sufficient liquid remains to continue cooking the rice.

Stir in the pork pieces and any juices from the platter, transfer to the oven, and cook, uncovered, until the rice is almost al dente, 10–12 minutes in a gas oven, 15–20 minutes electric. Remove to a warm spot, cover with foil, and let sit 5–10 minutes more. To "fry" the bottom layer of the rice, uncover the paella and place over high heat for about 2 minutes, until the rice begins to stick to the pan (be careful not to burn it).

Pork and Pomegranate Paella

(Paella de Magra y Granadina)

Pomegranates are closely associated with Spanish history and are a legacy of centuries of Moorish domination in Spain. The Moors were fond of sweet-and-sour flavors, and they planted pomegranate trees in Andalucía. In fact, the Andalusian city of Granada bears the same name as the pomegranate (granada in Spanish), perhaps in reference to the ruddy-colored brick used to build the Alhambra, the ethereal Moorish palace. Today the pomegranate remains the symbol of Granada, and its image appears as well in Spain's national coat of arms.

This is an outstanding paella of captivating flavor. The pork is marinated in a mixture of fresh pomegranate juice boiled down to a syrup, herbs, and spices, giving the meat and the paella a wonderful hint of sweetness, while the watercress with its slightly bitter edge is a perfect foil.

Buy pomegranates in the fall and freeze the seeds if you would like to have them on hand anytime. Bottled grenadine syrup, although ostensibly made from pomegranates, is more likely to be a mix of corn syrup, fruit flavors, and food coloring, but if you cannot find the real thing, substitute it for the fresh juice.

Serves 4 to 6

2 pomegranates or ¼ cup grenadine syrup diluted with ¼ cup water

1 bay leaf, crumbled

1 tablespoon rosemary leaves or ½ teaspoon dried

4 tablespoons minced parsley

1½ teaspoons ground cumin

8 cloves garlic, minced

Kosher or sea salt

Freshly ground pepper

¼ cup dry white wine

1 pound pork loin, cut in ½-inch cubes

About 5¾ cups chicken broth, canned or homemade (page 207)

¼ teaspoon crumbled thread saffron

8 tablespoons olive oil

1 medium onion, finely chopped

1½ cups finely chopped watercress (mostly leaves)

3 cups imported Spanish or Arborio short-grain rice

Cut the pomegranates in quarters, remove the seeds, and place in a food processor. Pulse for a few seconds, just long enough to release the juice. Strain, transfer to a small saucepan, and boil until reduced by half and slightly syrupy. (Omit this step if using grenadine syrup.) Let cool.

In a bowl, combine the pomegranate syrup, bay leaf, half of the rosemary, 2 tablespoons of the parsley, ¾ teaspoon of the cumin, half of the minced garlic, salt and pepper to taste, and the wine. Stir in the pork, cover, and marinate for 1 hour.

Remove the meat from the marinade, dry on paper towels, then sprinkle with salt. Combine the marinade in a large saucepan with the saffron and enough broth to make 6 cups. Keep hot over the lowest heat.

Preheat the oven to 400° F for gas oven, 450° F for electric.

Heat the oil in a paella pan measuring 17–18 inches at its widest point (or in a shallow casserole of a similar size), over 2 burners if necessary. Sauté the pork over high heat until lightly browned (it should not be fully cooked). Remove to a warm platter.

Add the onion and remaining garlic, and sauté until slightly softened. Stir in the watercress, the remaining rosemary, the remaining 2 tablespoons parsley, and ¾ teaspoon cumin, and cook 1 minute more. Add the rice and coat well with the pan mixture. Pour in all the hot broth and bring to a boil, stirring and rotating the pan occasionally. Taste for salt, continue to boil for about 3 minutes, then return the pork to the pan and boil about 2 minutes more, until the rice is no longer soupy but sufficient liquid remains to continue cooking the rice.

Transfer to the oven and cook, uncovered, until the rice is almost al dente, 10–12 minutes in a gas oven, 15–20 minutes electric. Remove to a warm spot, cover with foil, and let sit 5–10 minutes, until the rice is cooked to taste.

Rice with Pork, Potato, and Baked Eggs, Galician Style

(Arroz a la Gallega)

Start the preparation several hours in advance.

New potatoes mixed into the rice and eggs baked over the rice are delightful contrasts to the assertiveness of the paella's marinated pork. This paella is based on a traditional dish from Galicia, the region in Spain's northwestern corner where ancient Celtic traditions, like the playing of bagpipes, remain strong.

Serves 4

¾ pound boneless pork loin, cut in
    ½-inch cubes

¼ teaspoon kosher or sea salt

4 teaspoons sweet paprika,
    preferably Spanish smoked

6 cloves garlic, minced

1 small bay leaf, crumbled

3 cups chicken broth, canned or
    homemade (page 207)

⅛ teaspoon crumbled thread saffron

4 tablespoons olive oil

½ red bell pepper, finely chopped

½ green bell pepper, finely
    chopped

1 medium tomato, finely
    chopped

1 tablespoon minced parsley

⅛ teaspoon cayenne pepper, or to
    taste

1½ cups imported Spanish or
    Arborio short-grain rice

8 very small new potatoes
    (about 1½ inches), boiled and
    peeled

4 eggs

12–16 small asparagus spears,
    cooked

Pimiento strips

In a bowl, mix the pork with the salt, 2 teaspoons of the sweet paprika, garlic, and bay leaf. Marinate for several hours in the refrigerator.

Combine the broth and saffron in a pot and keep hot over the lowest heat.

Preheat the oven to 400° F for gas oven, 450° F for electric.

Heat the oil in a paella pan measuring 13 inches at its widest point (or in a shallow casserole of a similar size). Sauté the red and green peppers over medium-high heat until slightly softened. Add the pork and continue cooking until it loses its color (it should not be fully cooked). Remove the pork to a warm platter. Add the tomato and parsley, cook 1–2 minutes, then stir in the remaining 2 teaspoons sweet paprika and the cayenne.

Stir in the rice, coating it well with the pan mixture. Pour in the hot broth, bring to a boil, and boil 3 minutes, stirring occasionally. Add the reserved pork, taste for salt, and boil until the rice is no longer soupy but sufficient liquid remains to continue cooking the rice, about 5 minutes. Stir in the cooked potatoes. Break 1 egg at a time into a cup and slide over the rice, then garnish the rice with the cooked asparagus and the pimiento.

Transfer to the oven and cook, uncovered, until the rice is almost al dente and the eggs are set, 10–12 minutes in a gas oven, 15–20 minutes electric. Remove to a warm spot, cover with foil, and let sit about 5 minutes, until the rice is cooked to taste.

Pork, Chickpea, and Red Pepper Paella

(Paella con Magra, Garbanzos, y Pimientos Rojos)

Of all the great paellas at the fabulous La Dársena restaurant in Alicante, I particularly like this one in which red pepper becomes a key player. Instead of being finely chopped and disappearing into the rice, the peppers are cut in large pieces and only lightly cooked, so they retain their independent identity and give a touch of sweetness to the paella. Combined with pork and chickpeas, this is a special paella indeed.

Serves 4 to 6

¾ pound boneless pork loin, cut in ½-inch cubes

2 cloves garlic, mashed to a paste in a mortar or garlic press

3 tablespoons minced parsley

6 tablespoons olive oil

Kosher or sea salt

Freshly ground pepper

4 cups chicken broth, canned or homemade (page 207)

2½ cups canned chickpeas, drained and rinsed

¼ teaspoon crumbled thread saffron

2 large red bell peppers, cut in ¾-inch squares

10 cloves garlic, minced

2 tablespoons diced Spanish serrano ham or prosciutto, cut from a ¼-inch-thick slice

1 medium tomato, finely chopped

2 teaspoons paprika, preferably Spanish smoked

2 cups imported Spanish or Arborio short-grain rice

Combine the pork with the mashed garlic, 1 tablespoon of the parsley, 1 tablespoon of the oil, salt and pepper to taste. Let sit about 20 minutes.

Place the broth in a pot. Mash ½ cup of the chickpeas and add to the broth along with the saffron. Keep hot over the lowest heat.

Preheat the oven to 400° F for gas oven, 450° F for electric.

Heat the remaining 5 tablespoons oil in a paella pan measuring about 13 inches at its widest point (or in a shallow casserole of a similar size). Quickly brown the pork (it should not be fully cooked), then remove to a warm platter. Add the red peppers and sauté 1 minute over medium heat. Add the garlic, ham, tomato, and the remaining 2 tablespoons parsley. Sauté 2 minutes, then stir in the paprika, the pork, and any juices from the platter. Add the rice and coat well with the pan mixture. Pour in the hot broth, add the remaining 2 cups chickpeas, and taste for salt. Bring to a boil and continue boiling, stirring occasionally, until the rice is no longer soupy but sufficient liquid remains to continue cooking the rice, about 5 minutes.

Transfer to the oven and cook, uncovered, until the rice is almost al dente, 10–12 minutes in a gas oven, 15–20 minutes electric. Remove to a warm spot, cover with foil, and let sit 5–10 minutes, until the rice is cooked to taste.

Catalan-Style Paella

(Arroz a la Catalana)

The cooking of Catalunya, Spain's northeastern region that centers on the exciting city of Barcelona, features many beguiling main-course dishes based on the medieval use of honey, fruits, and nuts. Joining somewhat disparate ingredients into a single dish is the Catalan style, and many paellas certainly fall into that category. This rice includes almond and pine nuts. It may also call for chicken and seafood, but I prefer this version, which concentrates on pork products and artichokes.

Serves 6 to 8

2 tablespoons blanched slivered almonds

2 tablespoons pine nuts

4 cloves garlic, minced

4 tablespoons minced parsley

¼ teaspoon crumbled thread saffron

Kosher or sea salt

6 cups chicken broth, canned or homemade (page 207)

8 tablespoons olive oil

½ pound boneless pork loin, cut in ½-inch cubes

¼ pound diced Spanish serrano ham or prosciutto, cut from a ¼-inch-thick slice

½ pound lean, mildly spiced sausage such as Spanish *butifarra* or bratwurst

3 medium red bell peppers, finely chopped

2 medium onions, finely chopped

2 teaspoons sweet paprika, preferably Spanish smoked

2 medium tomatoes, finely chopped

3 cups imported Spanish or Arborio short-grain rice

6 tablespoons frozen or fresh peas

12 frozen artichoke hearts, cut in quarters

Pimiento strips for garnish

Preheat the oven to 350° F.

Spread the almonds and pine nuts on an oven tray and toast in the oven until golden, about 5 minutes. In a mortar or miniprocessor, mash as fine as possible the almonds, pine nuts, garlic, parsley, saffron, and ¼ teaspoon salt. Add about 2 teaspoons water and continue to mash to a paste. Stir in another 3 tablespoons water.

Pour the broth into a pot and keep hot over the lowest heat. Raise the oven to 400° F for gas oven, 450° F for electric.

Heat 2 tablespoons of the oil in a paella pan measuring 17–18 inches at its widest point (or in a shallow casserole of a similar size), over 2 burners if necessary. Sauté the pork, ham, and sausage over medium-high heat until lightly browned. Drain off most of the fat and oil. Add the remaining 6 tablespoons oil, the red peppers, and onions, and sauté until the vegetables are softened. Stir in the paprika and tomatoes, and cook 2 minutes. Lower the heat and cook about 15 minutes more.

Stir in the rice and coat well with the pan mixture. Pour in all the hot broth and bring to a boil. Taste for salt, add the mortar mixture, peas, and artichokes, and continue to boil, stirring and rotating the pan, until the rice is no longer soupy but sufficient liquid remains to continue cooking the rice, about 5 minutes.

Arrange the pimientos over the rice and transfer to the oven. Cook, uncovered, until the rice is almost al dente, 10–12 minutes in a gas oven, 15–20 minutes electric. Remove to a warm spot, cover with foil, and let sit 5–10 minutes, until the rice is cooked to taste.

Chorizo and Olive Paella "Santa Clara"

(Paella Monacal "Santa Clara")

Chorizo, the tasty Spanish sausage seasoned with garlic and paprika, usually plays a minor role in paella, but here it is the star. In supporting roles are capers, cured ham, and olives—both green and black—all contributing to the robust flavor of the rice. Snap peas or snow peas are a nice mellow contrast.

This recipe is based on one from the Clarisa nuns of the Santa Clara convent in Brivi-esca, province of Burgos, in the heart of Castile, which has no access to the sea. It is little wonder that this version of paella relies strictly on products of the land.

Serves 6 to 8

4 tablespoons coarsely chopped Spanish green olives

4 tablespoons coarsely chopped cured black olives (not California olives)

½ cup dry white wine

6 cups chicken broth, canned or homemade (page 207), or a mixture of chicken and beef broth

¼ teaspoon crumbled thread saffron

8 tablespoons olive oil

½ pound chorizo, preferably sweet, skinned and cut in ½-inch slices

1 medium onion, finely chopped

4 cloves garlic, minced

1 medium red bell pepper, finely chopped

¼ pound Spanish serrano ham or prosciutto, cut in ¼-inch slices and then diced

4 tablespoons minced parsley

3 cups imported Spanish or Arborio short-grain rice

Kosher or sea salt

2 dozen snap peas or snow peas

Place the green and black olives in a small saucepan with the wine and bring to a boil. Simmer 5 minutes. Drain and reserve.

Combine the broth and saffron in a pot and keep hot over the lowest heat.

Preheat the oven to 400° F for gas oven, 450° F for electric.

Heat the oil in a paella pan measuring 17–18 inches at its widest point (or in a shallow casserole of a similar size), over 2 burners if necessary. Sauté the chorizo for 1 minute, then add the onion, garlic, pepper, ham, and parsley, and sauté until the pepper is slightly softened.

Stir in the reserved olives and the rice, and coat the rice well with the pan mixture. Pour in the hot broth and bring to a boil, stirring and rotating the pan occasionally. Taste for salt and continue to boil until the rice is no longer soupy but sufficient liquid remains to continue cooking the rice, about 5 minutes. Stir in the snap peas.

Transfer to the oven and cook, uncovered, until the rice is almost al dente, 10–12 minutes in a gas oven, 15–20 minutes electric. Remove to a warm spot, cover with foil, and let sit 5–10 minutes, until the rice is cooked to taste.

Mushroom and Meatball Paella, La Dársena Style

(Arroz con Setas y Albóndigas La Dársena)

My husband and I journeyed to Alicante on the Valencian coast to visit the elegant La Dársena restaurant overlooking the city's port. We had heard that the restaurant's repertoire included fifty different paellas, and we assumed that a few were featured on any given day. When we arrived, we were astounded to find all fifty paellas there for the asking. We had entered paella heaven.

But paellas are typically prepared for a minimum of two, which would have limited us to just one of the fifty selections. Undeterred and to our waiter's astonishment, we ordered four paellas. All were perfectly executed by the restaurant's master paella chefs.

This paella from La Dársena is made in the Alicante style with dried sweet red peppers and paprika and is studded with pork and pine nut mini-meatballs.

Serves 4 to 5

4 cups chicken broth, canned or homemade (page 207)

2 sprigs parsley

1 dried sweet red peppers (*ñoras*; see Sources, page 215) or mild New Mexico pepper, or 1 fresh red bell pepper, split, cored, and seeded

10 cloves garlic, peeled

1/8 teaspoon crumbled thread saffron

2 medium tomatoes, chopped

2 tablespoons paprika, or 3 tablespoons if using fresh red pepper instead of dried

MEATBALLS

¾ pound (¾ cup) lean ground pork
1 egg
2 tablespoons minced parsley
1 teaspoon salt
3 tablespoons finely chopped pine
    nuts

¼ cup dried bread crumbs
1 clove garlic, minced
2 tablespoons chicken broth,
    canned or homemade
    (page 207)
Freshly ground pepper to taste

∼

4 tablespoons olive oil
1 medium red bell or
    elongated pepper, cut in
    ½-inch dice
¾ pound boneless pork loin, cut in
    ½-inch cubes
8 cloves garlic, minced

2 ounces mild-flavored mushrooms,
    preferably oyster, brushed clean,
    stems trimmed, and chopped
    (about ⅔ cup)
1½ cups imported Spanish or
    Arborio short-grain rice
2 egg whites, lightly beaten with a fork

Combine in a pot the broth, parsley, red pepper, peeled garlic, saffron, half of the chopped tomatoes, and the paprika. Bring to a boil and cook at a high simmer, uncovered, for 30 minutes. Strain, pushing through as much of the solids as possible, to make 3 cups.

Meanwhile, make the meatballs: In a bowl, combine all the meatball ingredients, shape into 1-inch balls, and reserve.

Keep the broth hot over the lowest heat. Preheat the oven to 400° F for gas oven, 450° F for electric.

Heat the oil in a paella pan measuring about 13 inches at its widest point (or in a shallow casserole of a similar size) and sauté the red pepper over medium-high heat until softened. Add the pork, stir to separate the pieces, and sauté until it loses its color. Add the remaining half of the chopped tomatoes, garlic, and mushrooms, and cook 1–2 minutes. Mix in the rice, coating it well with the pan mixture. Pour in the hot broth and bring to a boil.

Coat the meatballs with the egg whites and add to the pan. Taste for salt and continue to boil, stirring occasionally, until the rice is no longer soupy but sufficient liquid remains to continue cooking the rice, about 5 minutes.

Transfer to the oven and cook, uncovered, until the rice is almost al dente, 10–12 minutes in a gas oven, 15–20 minutes electric. Remove to a warm spot, cover with foil, and let sit 5–10 minutes, until the rice is cooked to taste.

Tino's Chickpea Stew Paella

(Arroz al Horno al Estilo de Tino)

Start the preparation one day in advance.

This classic rice dish is prepared in homes all over Valencia. It is a hearty meal and as down to earth as they come. Whereas paellas usually finish in the oven, Valencian "baked rice" dishes cook almost entirely in the oven. In essence, arroz al horno *is Spain's celebrated chickpea stew to which rice is added, so it requires more time than a typical paella. However, everything up to the point of adding the rice can be done several days in advance.*

This recipe was given to me by Tino Salcedo, a Valencian living in New York. It is his mother's version of this traditional dish and his favorite meal, laden with childhood memories of wonderful Sunday afternoon repasts. I highly recommend it.

Serves 4 to 6

⅓ cup dried chickpeas
1 pound beef bones
One ½-pound piece lean beef stew
    meat
½ pound lean meaty pork ribs,
    hacked in 1½-inch pieces with a
    heavy knife or by a butcher
1 medium onion
1 medium leek, very well washed
Two 1-inch cubes fresh or salt pork,
    or slab bacon (about 2 ounces)
Kosher or sea salt
1 head garlic, loose skin removed
¼ teaspoon crumbled thread saffron

4 tablespoons olive oil
¼ pound black sausage,
    preferably Spanish *morcilla*
    (see Sources, page 215)
1 medium potato, peeled and
    cut in ¼-inch slices
3 small tomatoes, cut in half
    crosswise
3 cloves garlic, minced
½ teaspoon sweet paprika,
    preferably Spanish
    smoked
2 cups imported Spanish or
    Arborio short-grain rice

Soak the chickpeas overnight in cold salted water to cover. Drain. In a large pot, combine 6 cups water, the beef bones, beef, pork ribs, onion, leek, salt pork, salt to taste, and chickpeas. Bring to a boil, cover, and simmer until the chickpeas are tender, about 2–2½ hours. Add the whole head of garlic and simmer 10 minutes more.

Strain, reserving the beef, garlic, ribs, and chickpeas. Cut the beef into 1-inch cubes.

Measure 4 cups of broth, taste for salt, combine with the saffron, and keep hot over the lowest heat.

Preheat the oven to 375° F for gas oven, 425° F for electric.

Heat the oil in a casserole, preferably fireproof Spanish earthenware, measuring about 15 inches. Sauté the black sausage for several minutes, then remove to a warm platter. Add the potato slices, sauté over medium heat until tender, then remove to the platter. Sauté the tomato halves briefly on both sides and remove to the platter. Sauté the reserved beef and ribs and the minced garlic, remove, and set aside. Stir in the paprika, chickpeas, and rice, and coat well with the pan mixture. Place the head of garlic at the center of the casserole and arrange the meats, tomatoes, potatoes, and sausage around it.

Pour in the hot broth, bring to a boil, and transfer to the oven. Bake 30–35 minutes (a few minutes more may be needed in an electric oven), until the rice is almost al dente. Remove to a warm spot, cover with foil, and let sit 5–10 minutes, until the rice is done to taste.

Cabbage and Chopped Meat Paella

(Arroz con Repollo y Carne Picada)

Although this rice is certainly made in the style of a paella, its ingredients—bacon, ground beef, cabbage, and ham—even though very Spanish—are not conventional additions to a paella. Nevertheless, I think it is excellent, a change of pace, and well worth trying.

Serves 4

3 cups chicken broth, canned or
 homemade (page 207)
⅛ teaspoon crumbled thread
 saffron
3 thin slices lean bacon
4 tablespoons olive oil
¾ pound lean ground beef
Salt
1 large onion, chopped
1 jalapeño pepper, cored, seeded,
 and minced (about 2 teaspoons)
2 tablespoons diced Spanish

serrano ham or prosciutto, cut
 from a ¼-inch-thick slice
¼ head (about ½ pound) cabbage,
 chopped
¼ teaspoon sweet paprika,
 preferably Spanish smoked
1½ cups imported Spanish or
 Arborio short-grain rice
1 bunch scallions (about ¼ pound),
 chopped
10 snow peas, cut in julienne
 strips

Preheat the oven to 400° F for gas oven, 450° F for electric.

Combine the broth and saffron in a saucepan and keep hot over the lowest heat.

In a paella pan measuring about 13 inches at its widest point (or in a shallow casserole of a similar size), fry the bacon strips until crisp. Drain on paper towels, crumble, and reserve. Pour off the fat or leave some in the pan for added flavor.

Add 2 tablespoons of the olive oil to the pan and sauté the ground beef, sprinkling with salt to taste and stirring and separating into small pieces, until it loses its color. Remove to a warm platter. Add the remaining 2 tablespoons oil and sauté the onion, pepper, and ham until the vegetables are softened. Add the cabbage and cook briefly until slightly wilted, then stir in the paprika. Add the rice and coat well with the pan mixture.

Pour in the broth, add the scallions, ground beef, and half of the bacon, and bring to a boil. Taste for salt and continue to boil, stirring occasionally, until the rice is no longer soupy but sufficient liquid remains to continue cooking the rice, about 5 minutes.

Transfer to the oven and cook 10–12 minutes in a gas oven, 15–20 minutes electric, until the rice is almost al dente. Remove to a warm spot, cover with foil, and let sit 5–10 minutes, until the rice is cooked to taste. Sprinkle with the julienned snow peas and the remaining bacon before serving. ·

HORCHATA:
VALENCIA'S SINGULAR ICY COLD REFRESHMENT

When I first arrived in Spain so many summers ago, my very first taste of the country was a glass of chilled *horchata* at an outdoor café. To this day it is my favorite summertime drink and for me an integral part of summers in Spain.

Creamy white with a sweet nutty flavor that somewhat resembles coconut but otherwise defies description, *horchata* is Valencia's favorite hot weather thirst quencher. It is made from the chufa (tiger nut), a small root resembling a peanut-size potato that is native to Africa and more specifically, some say, to a desert region of the Sudan called Chuf, or Chufi.

Legend tells that the Christian conqueror of Valencia, Jaime El Conquistador, was inspecting his newly won lands one fiery hot summer day and stopped at a farmhouse to rest. An Arab girl offered him a local drink that so impressed him that he was heard to exclaim (in medieval Spanish), "Aixo es or, xata" (This is gold, girl), which eventually was abridged to *horchata.*

To make *horchata,* chufas are soaked in water, ground, strained, then mixed with sugar. The resulting beverage is served chilled to a slush and is sipped leisurely by throngs of Valencians who flock to outdoor cafés on warm summer evenings.

Horchata is a fresh product that must be kept cold and therefore was once found exclusively in the Valencia region. Today it is available in most major Spanish cities (it is especially popular in Madrid) and has even arrived on our shores (see Sources, page 215) in long-life containers. One sip and I am instantly transported, in Proustian fashion, to that outdoor café in Spain, where I first fell in love with *horchata* so long ago.

Lamb and Red Pepper Paella

(Paella de Cordero Chilindrón)

Cordero chilindrón—lamb and red pepper stew—is a celebrated dish from the northeast interior region of Aragón, a mountainous area that dips into a broad valley around the grand Ebro River. Shepherds tending their flocks are a common sight, and the red peppers that grow in the Ebro valley are famous for their quality and sweetness. It seems only natural that lamb and peppers would join forces to create a regional specialty.

Similiar ingredients make a tasty paella. Herbs, cumin, saffron, and a broth enriched with mashed chickpeas season the rice, and tomato sliced over the paella is also a fine flavor accent. Since the lamb for this paella is not stewed, it is important to use meat from a tender quick-cooking cut, preferably the leg.

Serves 6

1⅓ cups canned chickpeas

6½ cups chicken broth, canned or homemade (page 207)

12 cloves garlic, coarsely chopped

1 medium onion, peeled

4 sprigs parsley

2 sprigs rosemary or ¼ teaspoon dried

2 sprigs thyme or ¼ teaspoon dried

¼ teaspoon dried oregano

1 bay leaf

½ teaspoon ground cumin

¼ teaspoon crumbled thread saffron

½ cup dry white wine

8 tablespoons olive oil

1½ pounds boneless leg of lamb, cut in ½- to ¾-inch cubes

Kosher or sea salt

2 medium red bell peppers, cored, seeded, and cut in ½-inch cubes

1 small onion, finely chopped

1 medium tomato, finely chopped

2 tablespoons brandy

3 cups imported Spanish or Arborio short-grain rice

1 pimiento, cut in ½-inch strips

Twelve ¼-inch slices tomato, cut from medium-size tomatoes

2 tablespoons minced parsley

Drain the chickpeas and reserve the liquid. Mash ⅔ cup of the chickpeas through a strainer into a pot, and combine with the broth, reserved liquid, garlic, the whole onion, parsley sprigs, rosemary, thyme, oregano, bay leaf, cumin, and saffron. Bring to a boil, cover, and simmer 20 minutes. Strain and measure 5½ cups. Stir in the wine to make 6 cups of liquid. Keep hot over the lowest heat.

Preheat the oven to 400° F for gas oven, 450° F for electric.

Heat the oil in a paella pan measuring 17–18 inches at its widest point (or in a shallow casserole of a similar size), over 2 burners if necessary. Sauté the lamb over high heat, sprinkling with salt to taste, until lightly brown (it should not be fully cooked). Remove to a warm platter. Add the red peppers and chopped onion, and sauté over medium-high heat until the vegetables are slightly softened. Stir in the chopped tomato and brandy, and cook away the liquid. Add the rice and coat well with the pan mixture. Pour in the hot broth and bring to a boil. Add the remaining ⅔ cup chickpeas, taste for salt, and continue to boil, stirring and rotating the pan, about 2 minutes. Stir in the lamb and boil 3 minutes more, until the rice is no longer soupy but sufficient liquid remains to continue cooking the rice.

Arrange the pimiento strips and sliced tomatoes over the rice. Transfer to the oven and cook, uncovered, 10–12 minutes in a gas oven, 15–20 minutes electric, until the rice is almost al dente. Remove to a warm spot, cover with foil, and let sit 5–10 minutes, until the rice is cooked to taste. Sprinkle with the minced parsley and serve.

Lamb, Lentil, and Eggplant Paella

(Arroz de Cordero, Lentejas, y Berenjena)

The ingredients in this paella are typically Spanish but with a decidedly Moorish accent, especially in the use of cumin and cilantro.

Serves 6 to 8

1 pound eggplant, skin on and cut in ½-inch cubes

Kosher or sea salt

6 cups chicken broth, canned or homemade (page 207)

¼ teaspoon crumbled thread saffron

8 tablespoons olive oil

1½ pounds boneless leg of lamb, cut in ½-inch cubes

1 small onion, finely chopped

8 cloves garlic, minced

1 green bell pepper, finely chopped

1 medium tomato, finely chopped

2 tablespoons minced parsley

1 cup cooked lentils, drained and rinsed

½ teaspoon dried oregano

½ teaspoon ground cumin

3 cups imported Spanish or Arborio short-grain rice

2 tablespoons chopped cilantro leaves

Place the eggplant in a colander and sprinkle with salt. Let sit 20 minutes. Pat dry with paper towels.

Combine the broth and saffron in a pot and keep hot over the lowest heat.

Preheat the oven to 400° F for gas oven, 450° F for electric.

Heat the oil in a paella pan measuring 17–18 inches at its widest point (or in a shallow casserole of a similar size), over 2 burners if necessary. Quickly sauté the lamb until it loses its color, turning and sprinkling with salt. Remove to a warm platter (it should not be fully cooked).

Add the onion, garlic, and pepper to the pan and sauté until slightly softened. Add the eggplant, sauté 1 minute, then add the tomato, parsley, lentils, oregano, and cumin. Stir in the rice and coat well with the pan mixture. Pour in the hot broth and bring to a boil. Taste for salt. Boil about 2 minutes, stirring and rotating the pan occasionally. Stir in the reserved lamb and boil 3 minutes more, until the rice is no longer soupy but sufficient liquid remains to continue cooking the rice.

Transfer to the oven and cook 10–12 minutes in a gas oven, 15–20 minutes electric, until the rice is almost al dente. Remove from the oven, cover with foil, and let sit 5–10 minutes. Sprinkle with the cilantro before serving.

Summer rice fields south of Valencia.

Rice and other grains at Valencia's Central Market.

Paella ingredients.

Detail, Chorizo
and Olive Paella
"Santa Clara."

Laborers' cottage's (*barracas*), Valencia.

Paella fest for five hundred, Alcora, Castellón de la Plana.

Paella over open fire,
restaurant Racó d'Olla,
El Palmar, Valencia.

Traditional Valencian paella.

Preparing paella at La Pepica restaurant, Valencia.

Seafood paellas in final stage of preparation, La Pepica.

Over-sized paella pan for a local Valencia festival.

Black Squid Paella
(right and below).

Detail, Mixed
Seafood Paella.

Bean-Pebbled Paella.

Rabbit, Spinach, and Artichoke Paella

(Paella de Conejo, Espinacas, y Alcachofas)

Spinach adds an interesting element to this paella, and when combined with artichokes and rabbit, you have a rice of very fine flavor. This paella is very easy to prepare—the ingredients are limited and there is little chopping to do. It is a traditional dish of Gandía in the province of Valencia.

Serves 4 to 5

One 2½-pound rabbit or small
   chicken, all skin and fat removed
Kosher or sea salt
5 cups chicken broth, canned or
   homemade (page 207)
¼ teaspoon crumbled thread
   saffron
5 tablespoons olive oil
4 cloves garlic, minced

1 medium tomato, skinned, seeded,
   and finely chopped
½ pound spinach, thick stems
   trimmed, washed, very well
   dried, and chopped (about
   6 cups)
2½ cups imported Spanish or
   Arborio short-grain rice
8 frozen artichoke hearts, quartered

Cut the rabbit into 2-inch pieces, discarding the bony tips of the legs. Sprinkle well with salt.

Combine the broth and saffron, and keep hot over the lowest heat.

Preheat the oven to 400° F for gas oven, 450° F for electric.

Heat the oil in a paella pan measuring 17–18 inches at its widest point (or a shallow casserole of a similar size), over 2 burners if necessary. Sauté the rabbit over high heat for 5 minutes, turning once. Remove to a warm platter. Add the garlic, tomato, and spinach to the pan and sauté until the spinach is wilted. Stir in the rice, coating it well with the pan mixture. Pour in the hot broth and add the artichokes. Bring to a boil, taste for salt, and continue to boil until the rice is no longer soupy but sufficient liquid remains to continue cooking the rice, about 5 minutes. Stir in the rabbit pieces and any juices from the platter.

Transfer to the oven and cook, uncovered, until the rice is almost al dente, 10–12 minutes in a gas oven, 15–20 minutes electric. Remove to a warm spot, cover with foil, and let sit 5–10 minutes, until the rice is cooked to taste.

Mixed Meat and Seafood Paellas

Pork, Sausage, Chicken, and Seafood Paella

Fresh Tuna and Rabbit Paella

Catalan Mar y Montaña Paella

SAFFRON : THREADS OF GOLD

Since time immemorial, saffron has been revered for its haunting flavor and the appealing yellow color it gives to foods and beverages. The Greeks, the Romans, and the ancient Persians all prized saffron, but when the Dark Ages descended over the civilized world, saffron became an out-of-reach and needless luxury, and it all but disappeared.

The Moors rescued saffron from oblivion, reintroducing it to Europe by way of Spain in the eighth century. They found an ideal microclimate in southern Castile, not far from Valencia, to grow the purple autumn crocus from which *zafaran*—an Arab word referring to saffron's yellow color—was obtained.

Most of the world's saffron is produced in Spain, and it is a spice more valuable than gold—and for good reason. Saffron is very simply the stamens of the saffron crocus, and for just a few days in October the plants push forth, spreading a vast purple carpet over the parched earth. I was privileged to be in the closely guarded saffron fields at the right moment, and I will never forget that splendid sight.

Young boys carrying large wicker baskets expertly plucked the flowers, one by one, while they were still wet with dew. They took their prized harvest home, where other family members awaited to remove the three stamens in each flower and quickly roast them to preserve optimum quality. More than ten thousand flowers will yield no more than an ounce of dried saffron. Because the labor is intensive, entire villages—including children and elders—work long hours to bring in the crop. The reward is a treasure that reaches over $6,000 a pound and its price continues to spiral upward. What is not sold is stored under mattresses— a far better hedge against inflation than a savings account.

Despite its astounding price, a small amount of saffron is all that is ever necessary for any cooking needs (its intense aroma and pronounced flavor become overpowering if overused). But saffron really does make a difference—albeit a subtle one—in any number of dishes and most especially in paella, and I would not be without it in my kitchen. Beware, however, of paellas that are bright orange. They have been artificially colored; real saffron turns rice a pale yellow. Saffron's high cost, unfortunately, often results in money-saving shortcuts and sometimes leads to downright fraudulent practices, like mixing or substituting saffron for stamens and petals from other flowers and adding moisture to increase weight. The best insurance of quality is buying saffron from a trustworthy dealer.

Pork, Sausage, Chicken, and Seafood Paella

(Paella Mixta)

Although this is by far the most popular paella in American Spanish restaurants, in paella's homeland it comes close to heresy. Valencians don't believe in mixing fish and meat (and certainly not chorizo) into one paella; they prefer that each special ingredient shines on its own.

This is perhaps being a little extreme, for mixed paella is very tasty indeed and can be found on menus in Valencia, albeit mostly for the tourist trade. But the more I have learned about paella and the more paellas I have eaten, I tend to agree that by mixing disparate ingredients into one paella, none of the ingredients stands out or gives its own character to the rice. Having said this, here is an excellent recipe for a typical mixed paella (in many restaurants erroneously called Paella a la Valenciana). Once you have mastered the techniques of paella making, you can vary it as you will—perhaps arranging lobster and/or mussels over the rice for added flavor and visual impact. The lemon wedges, besides giving an attractive appearance, can be—and should be—squeezed over the rice.

Serves 6 to 8

6 cloves garlic, minced

2 tablespoons minced parsley

¼ teaspoon crumbled thread saffron

Kosher or sea salt

One small chicken or 2- to 2½-pound rabbit

¼ pound boneless pork loin, cut in ½-inch cubes

½ pound squid, cleaned, cut in ½-inch rings, and tentacles halved

½ pound monkfish, grouper, or other firm-fleshed fish, skin removed and cut in ½-inch cubes

12–16 extra-large shrimp in their shells

¼ pound chorizo, preferably sweet, cut in ¼-inch slices

6 cups clam juice, chicken broth, canned or homemade (page 207), or fish broth, canned or homemade (page 208)

8 tablespoons olive oil

1 onion, finely chopped

1 red bell pepper, finely chopped

1 medium tomato, finely chopped

2 teaspoons paprika, preferably Spanish smoked

3 cups imported Spanish or Arborio short-grain rice

½ cup frozen or fresh peas

1½–2 dozen small mussels (optional), cleansed (page 10)

Lemon wedges

In a mortar or miniprocessor, mash to a paste the garlic, parsley, saffron, and ⅛ teaspoon salt. Set aside.

Cut the chicken wings in 2 parts, discarding the tip. Chop off the bony end of the legs. Cut the rest of the chicken into quarters; then with kitchen shears cut into 1½-inch pieces. Sprinkle all over with salt the chicken, pork, squid, monkfish, and shrimp in their shells.

Preheat the oven to 400° F for gas oven, 450° F for electric. Pour the broth into a pot and keep hot over the lowest heat.

Heat 6 tablespoons of the oil in a paella pan measuring 17–18 inches at its widest point (or in a shallow casserole of a similar size), over 2 burners if necessary. Briefly sauté the shrimp in their shells over high heat and remove to a warm platter (they should not be fully cooked). Sauté the chicken until brown but not fully cooked. Remove to the platter. Add the pork, monkfish, and chorizo, cook 1–2 minutes, and remove to the platter. Add the squid, sauté 1 minute, and remove. Add the remaining 2 tablespoons oil, mix in the onion and red pepper, and cook until they are slightly softened. Stir in the tomato, cook 1–2 minutes, then stir in the paprika and rice, coating it well with the pan mixture.

Pour in the hot broth and bring to a boil. Add the mortar mixture, taste for salt, and continue to boil about 3 minutes, stirring and rotating the pan occasionally. Add the reserved monkfish, chorizo, pork, squid, and the peas, and boil about 2 minutes more, until the rice is no longer soupy but enough liquid remains to continue cooking the rice.

Arrange the chicken, shrimp, and optional mussels over the rice and transfer to the oven. Cook, uncovered, 10–12 minutes in a gas oven, 15–20 minutes electric, until the rice is almost al dente. Remove to a warm spot, cover with foil, and let sit 5–10 minutes, until the rice is cooked to taste. Garnish with lemon wedges.

Fresh Tuna and Rabbit Paella
(Paella de Atún y Conejo)

Tuna and rabbit (or chicken) are a natural pair since tuna has a meaty taste and consistency that bridges the gap between surf and turf. A broth well seasoned with herbs and plenty of paprika is one of the reasons for this paella's great taste.

Serves 6

16 cloves garlic, minced
2 tablespoons minced parsley
1½ teaspoons thyme leaves or
    ¼ teaspoon dried
¼ teaspoon dried oregano
Freshly ground pepper to
    taste
Kosher or sea salt
2 pimientos, chopped
4 teaspoons paprika, preferably
    Spanish smoked
½ teaspoon ground cumin
½ cup dry white wine
1 pound boneless rabbit or
    boneless, skinless chicken
    (preferably thigh meat), cut in
    ½-inch cubes

1 pound fresh tuna, cut in ½-inch
    cubes
5½ cups chicken broth,
    canned or homemade
    (page 207)
¼ teaspoon crumbled thread
    saffron
8 tablespoons olive oil
1 medium onion, finely
    chopped
2 medium tomatoes,
    skinned, seeded, and
    chopped
3 cups imported Spanish or
    Arborio short-grain rice

In a mortar or miniprocessor, mash to a paste the garlic, parsley, thyme, oregano, pepper, and ¼ teaspoon salt. Add the pimientos, paprika, and cumin, and mash again. Stir in the wine. Sprinkle the rabbit and tuna pieces well with salt and let sit 10 minutes at room temperature.

Preheat the oven to 400° F for gas oven, 450° F for electric. Combine the broth with the saffron and keep hot over the lowest heat.

Heat the oil in a paella pan measuring 17–18 inches at its widest point (or in a shallow casserole of a similar size), over 2 burners if necessary, until very hot. Add the rabbit and tuna and brown lightly (they should not be fully cooked). Remove to a warm platter. Lower the heat, add the onion, and cook slowly until soft but not brown. Add the tomatoes and continue cooking slowly 5 minutes more.

Stir in the rice and coat well with the pan mixture, then add the mortar mixture and pour in the hot broth. Bring to a boil, taste for salt, and continue boiling about 3 minutes, stirring and rotating the pan. Add the tuna, chicken, and any juices from the platter, and boil until the rice is no longer soupy but sufficient liquid remains to continue cooking the rice, about 2 minutes.

Transfer to the oven and cook, uncovered, 10–12 minutes in a gas oven, 15–20 minutes electric, until the rice is almost al dente. Remove to a warm spot, cover with foil, and let sit about 5 minutes.

Return to the top of the stove and cook over high heat until the bottom of the rice is brown and crisp (be careful not to burn it).

Catalan Mar y Montaña Paella

Spain's version of "surf and turf" from Catalunya is translated here into a rice dish that incorporates chicken, shrimp, and the typical Catalan mash (picada) of nuts, garlic, and parsley for an added blast of flavor. Mushrooms and a touch of brandy also contribute to the paella's exceptional taste.

Serves 6

5 cups chicken broth, canned or homemade (page 207)

¼ teaspoon crumbled thread saffron

1½ teaspoons thyme leaves or ¼ teaspoon dried

¼ teaspoon dried oregano

1 bay leaf

4 medium leeks, very well washed and trimmed

¾ pound small to medium shrimp in their shells

One 3-pound chicken, breast and thigh only

Kosher or sea salt

½ cup dry white wine

8 tablespoons olive oil

4 tablespoons blanched slivered almonds

8 cloves garlic, minced

2 tablespoons minced parsley

2 tablespoons brandy

1 medium onion, finely chopped

1 medium red bell pepper, finely chopped

½ pound oyster or other mild-flavored mushrooms, brushed clean, stems trimmed and chopped

2 medium tomatoes, finely chopped

3 cups imported Spanish or Arborio short-grain rice

In a large pot, combine the broth, saffron, thyme, oregano, bay leaf, and 1½ cups water. Cut off the green portion of the leeks and add to the broth. Mince the white portion and reserve. Shell the shrimp and add the shells to the broth. Bring the broth to a boil, cover, and simmer 30 minutes.

Cut the chicken with kitchen shears into 2-inch pieces. Sprinkle the shrimp and chicken all over with salt.

Preheat the oven to 400° F for gas oven, 450° F for electric.

Strain the broth and measure to 5½ cups. Add the wine and keep hot over the lowest heat.

Heat the oil in a paella pan measuring 17–18 inches at its widest point (or in a shallow casserole of a similar size), over 2 burners if necessary, and sauté the almonds until golden. Remove to a mortar or miniprocessor and mash to a paste with half of the minced garlic, ¼ teaspoon salt, and the parsley. Gradually mash in the brandy. Set aside.

Reheat the paella pan and sauté the chicken over high heat, turning once, about 5 minutes, until brown (it should not be fully cooked). Remove to a warm platter. Add the shrimp and sauté, turning once, less than a minute, and remove to the platter. Reduce the heat and stir in the pepper, onion, minced leek, and remaining minced garlic, and sauté until the onion is slightly softened. Stir in the mushrooms and the tomato and cook 2 minutes more, then stir in half of the mortar mixture.

Add the rice and coat well with the pan mixture. Pour in all the hot broth and bring to a boil. Taste for salt and continue boiling, stirring and rotating the pan occasionally, until the rice is no longer soupy but sufficient liquid remains to continue cooking the rice, about 5 minutes. Stir in the rest of the mortar mixture and the shrimp.

Arrange the chicken pieces over the rice and transfer to the oven. Cook, uncovered, until the rice is almost al dente, 10–12 minutes in a gas oven, 15–20 minutes electric. Remove to a warm spot, cover with foil, and let sit 5–10 minutes, until the rice is cooked to taste.

Vegetable Paellas

Tricolor Paella with Cheese, Anchovies, and Almonds

Spinach, Chickpea, and Pine Nut Paella

Bean-Pebbled Paella

Brown Rice, Vegetable, and Pine Nut Paella

Vegetable Paella with Spicy Garlic Sauce

Eggplant, Olive, Anchovy, and Caper Paella

Potpourri of Mushrooms Paella

Green and Yellow Squash Paella with Pesto

Baked Rice with Garlic, Potatoes, and Chickpeas

PIQUILLOS, ÑORAS, AND SMOKED PAPRIKA: PRODUCTS OF SPAIN'S DISTINCTIVE RED PEPPERS

Spaniards have been inordinately fond of peppers—red and green, sweet and hot, fresh and dried—ever since Columbus discovered this native American vegetable in the New World, where it had been cultivated for thousands of years. The hot pepper he came upon had the bite associated with Far Eastern peppercorns, and since Columbus believed he had found a westerly route to the East, he assumed he was tasting a variety of black pepper. To this day, in English and in Spanish, the word for pepper as a spice and pepper as a vegetable is the same, distinguished in Spanish only by a change of vowel: *pimienta* for black pepper, and *pimiento* for all vegetables of the Capsicum family.

But Spain's true love is the sweet red pepper, which besides being a common fresh ingredient in Spanish cooking—especially in paellas—is equally popular when roasted and sold in jars. In particular, the *piquillo* pepper from Navarra is so extraordinary that it has been granted its very own denomination of origin, for it is strictly an artisan product.

Piquillos are delicious straight from the jar, although I particularly like them lightly sautéed with garlic and olive oil as a side course or as an appetizer (you will find them featured in this book in Piquillo Pepper Salad with Raisins and Pine Nuts). They also make elegant main courses when filled with meat, seafood, vegetables, or cheese and bathed in a classic Spanish sauce, like red pepper purée or squid ink sauce. With *piquillos* you can let your imagination take flight, as chefs in Spain have long done.

Two other varieties of Spanish sweet red peppers are often dried and used as distinctive seasonings. They are called *ñoras* in paella's homeland (you will find them recommended in many paella recipes in this book) and *pimientos choriceros* in the north of Spain, where they are essential to the sauce of such regional dishes as *bacalao a la vizcaína*. Both give a unique musky flavor and a rusty red color to sauces and broths.

Paprika (*pimentón*) is similar in flavor to these dried peppers and is an ingredient in almost every kind of paella. Spain's best paprikas come from the central western region of Extremadura and also have their specific denomination of origin. They have a tantalizing smoky flavor, a result of slow drying over oak fires, and enhance paellas as no ordinary paprika can.

If you want your Spanish cooking to be truly authentic, keep on hand, as I always do, *piquillo* peppers, *ñoras*, and Spanish smoked paprika (see Sources, page 215), exceptional red pepper products unique to Spain.

Tricolor Paella with Cheese, Anchovies, and Almonds

(Paella Tricolor con Queso, Anchoa, y Almendra)

Cheese, anchovies, and almonds lend such a subtle taste to this rice that I doubt you can identify them as ingredients. But there is no question that they provide the flavors that make this meatless paella exceptional. Tricolor refers to the green, red, and yellow peppers that are mixed into the rice and also to the three colors of peppers used as a festive garnish.

Serves 6

4 tablespoons slivered almonds

2 medium red bell peppers

2 medium yellow bell peppers

2 medium green bell peppers

4 tablespoons minced parsley

4 cloves garlic, chopped

Kosher or sea salt

6 anchovy fillets, preferably jarred, chopped

¼ cup grated, well-cured Spanish Manchego or Parmesan cheese

6 cups chicken broth, canned or homemade (page 207), or vegetable broth, canned or homemade (page 208)

¼ teaspoon crumbled thread saffron

8 tablespoons olive oil

2 medium onions, finely chopped

1 medium tomato, finely chopped

¼ cup frozen or fresh peas

3 cups imported Spanish or Arborio short-grain rice

Preheat the oven to 350° F.

Place the almonds on a baking sheet in the oven for about 8 minutes, until golden. Remove to a mortar or miniprocessor. Turn the oven up to 550° F. Arrange the red, yellow, and green peppers in a roasting pan and roast about 20 minutes, until the skins are brown and separated from the flesh, turning once.

Meanwhile, add to the almonds in the mortar or miniprocessor the parsley, garlic, and ¼ teaspoon salt, and mash as fine as possible. Mash in the anchovies, adding 2 teaspoons broth or water to facilitate the process. Add the cheese and 2 more teaspoons water, and mash some more.

When the peppers are done, remove from the oven and cover with a towel until cool. Skin, core, seed, and cut 1 pepper of each color into ½-inch strips. Chop the remaining peppers. Lower oven temperature to 400° F for gas, 450° F for electric.

Combine the broth with the saffron and keep hot over the lowest heat. Heat the oil in a paella pan measuring 17–18 inches at its widest point (or in a shallow casserole of similar size), over 2 burners if necessary. Sauté the onions over medium heat until softened. Raise the heat and add the tomato, peas, and chopped peppers, and cook about 3 minutes.

Stir in the rice and coat well with the pan mixture, then pour in the broth and bring to a boil. Stir in the mortar mixture, taste for salt, and boil, stirring and rotating the pan occasionally, until the rice is no longer soupy but enough liquid remains to continue cooking the rice, about 5 minutes.

Arrange the pepper strips in a starburst pattern over the rice and transfer to the oven for 10–12 minutes in a gas oven, 15–20 minutes electric, until the rice is almost al dente. Remove to a warm spot, cover with foil, and let sit 5–10 minutes, until the rice is cooked to taste.

Spinach, Chickpea, and Pine Nut Paella

(Paella de Espinacas, Garbanzos, y Piñones)

This simple vegetable paella makes a satisfying meal and is made special by a substantial amount of spinach, the crunch of pine nuts, and the distinctive taste of cumin.

Serves 6 to 8

¾ cup canned chickpeas, drained
    and rinsed (reserve can liquid)
About 5 cups chicken broth,
    canned or homemade (page 207)
    or vegetable broth, canned or
    homemade (page 208)
½ cup dry white wine
¼ teaspoon crumbled thread
    saffron
8 tablespoons olive oil
4 tablespoons pine nuts
16 cloves garlic, minced
1 small onion, finely chopped
1 large red pepper, finely chopped

2 medium tomatoes, finely chopped
2 tablespoons minced parsley
½ pound spinach leaves, washed,
    well dried, and chopped
    (about 8 cups)
4 teaspoons sweet paprika,
    preferably Spanish smoked
1 tablespoon thyme leaves or
    ½ teaspoon dried
½ teaspoon ground cumin
½ teaspoon dried oregano
3 cups imported Spanish or
    Arborio short-grain rice

Preheat the oven to 400° F for gas oven, 450° F for electric.

Combine in a pot the chickpea liquid and broth to make 5½ cups. Add the wine and saffron, and keep hot over the lowest heat.

Heat the oil in a paella pan measuring 17–18 inches at its widest point (or in a shallow casserole of a similar size), over 2 burners if necessary. Add the pine nuts and brown lightly, then add the garlic, onion, and red pepper, and cook over medium-high heat until the vegetables are slightly wilted. Add the tomatoes, parsley, and spinach, and sauté 2–3 minutes, until the spinach has cooked down. Stir in the paprika, thyme, cumin, and oregano, then the rice, coating it well with the pan mixture.

Pour in the hot broth and bring to a boil. Taste for salt, add the chickpeas, and continue to boil, stirring and rotating the pan occasionally, until the rice is no longer soupy but sufficient liquid remains to continue cooking the rice, about 5 minutes.

Transfer to the oven and cook, uncovered, until the rice is almost al dente, 10–12 minutes in a gas oven, 15–20 minutes electric. Remove to a warm spot, cover with foil, and let sit 5–10 minutes, until the rice is cooked to taste.

CLEMENTINES:
VALENCIAN GOODNESS FROM THE ORCHARDS

Valencia is an ideal region for citrus trees, and they have flourished here for centuries. The Moors loved the orange tree for its ornamental beauty and fragrant flowers and planted orange trees all over southern Spain, where they still grace the streets and patios of Andalucía's cities and villages.

Sweet oranges were introduced to Spain in the eighteenth century, and they changed the economy and the appearance of Valencia. It is spectacular indeed to see citric trees with their lustrous deep green leaves and bright orange and yellow fruits extending as far as the eye can see across the landscape of northern Valencia.

Spaniards brought oranges to the New World by way of Franciscan friars, who found in California and Florida climates equally suited to growing citric fruits. The clementine, however, is a relatively new fruit, little more than a century old, and is the result of a hybrid tangerine developed by a monk named Clemente in his monastery's gardens. Once the fruit was perfected some thirty years ago, its popularity soared.

I always look forward to the arrival of November, when boxes of clementines from Spain fill supermarkets and specialty shops in the United States. The clementine gains new devotees every year, as Americans learn about this "fun fruit" that peels in a flash, has no seeds, and is intensely sweet and juicy.

Curiously, the clementine only finds the precise conditions it requires in the unique microclimate that exists in the Valencian region and more specifically in the province of Castellón de la Plana. There, the right soil and humidity, coupled with mild temperatures, strong sunlight, and cool winter evenings, are ideal for growing clementines. In addition, costly hand picking must take place over a period of several months, since clementines do not ripen simultaneously. Because so many factors go into growing seedless clementines, no other country has as yet been able to match the superb quality of clementines from Valencia.

Bean-Pebbled Paella

(Arroz Empedrat)

A very colorful rice with a pebbled appearance (thus its name), obtained from the abundance of different-colored beans that make up this paella (the black beans are particularly striking). Aside from a touch of cured ham, this is strictly a vegetable paella made especially tasty by the addition of Swiss chard and cumin.

Serves 6 to 8

⅔ cup each canned chickpeas, pinto beans, red beans, and black beans (reserve all the can liquid except from the black beans)

About 4½ cups chicken broth, canned or homemade (page 207) or vegetable broth, canned or homemade (page 208)

¼ teaspoon crumbled thread saffron

8 tablespoons olive oil

2 bunches scallions (about ½ pound), trimmed and finely chopped

12 cloves garlic, minced

2 red bell peppers, finely chopped

3 cups well-washed, dried, and chopped Swiss chard leaves

6 tablespoons (about 6 ounces) diced Spanish serrano or prosciutto cured ham cut from a ¼-inch-thick slice

1 medium tomato, finely chopped

2 tablespoons minced parsley

2 teaspoons sweet paprika, preferably Spanish smoked

1 teaspoon ground cumin

3 cups imported Spanish or Arborio short-grain rice

Kosher or sea salt

Preheat the oven to 400° F for gas oven, 450° F for electric.

Drain the beans and reserve the liquid from all the cans except the black beans. Rinse the beans. Combine the bean liquid in a pot with enough broth to make 6 cups. Add the saffron and keep hot over the lowest heat.

Heat the oil in a paella pan measuring 17–18 inches at its widest point (or in a shallow casserole of a similar size), over 2 burners if necessary. Sauté the scallions, garlic, red peppers, Swiss chard, and ham over medium heat until the peppers are slightly softened. Add the tomato and parsley, and cook 1–2 minutes, then add the paprika and cumin.

Stir in the rice and coat well with the pan mixture. Pour in the hot broth and bring to a boil. Add the beans, taste for salt, and continue to boil, stirring and rotating the pan occasionally, until the rice is no longer soupy but sufficient liquid remains to continue cooking the rice, about 5 minutes.

Transfer to the oven and cook, uncovered, 10–12 minutes in a gas oven, 15–20 minutes electric, until the rice is almost al dente. Remove to a warm spot, cover with foil, and let sit 5–10 minutes, until the rice is cooked to taste.

Brown Rice, Vegetable, and Pine Nut Paella

(Arroz Integral Hortelano con Piñones)

Brown rice makes an excellent paella, but the cooking method is somewhat different and lengthier than for other paellas. The rice must first be partially cooked and then transferred to a paella pan where it continues to cook with all the other ingredients. Despite the additional preparation time, this is a most satisfying paella, rich in flavor, moist, and filled with vegetables. The toasted pine nuts highlight the natural nuttiness of the rice.

Serves 6

2½ cups imported Spanish or other short-grain brown rice

8 cups chicken broth, canned or homemade (page 207) or vegetable broth, canned or homemade (page 208)

¼ teaspoon crumbled thread saffron

8 tablespoons olive oil

½ cup pine nuts

2 red bell peppers, finely chopped

2 bunches (about ½ pound) scallions, trimmed and chopped

6 cloves garlic, minced

2 small to medium tomatoes, skinned, seeded, and finely chopped

4 tablespoons minced parsley

1 teaspoon sweet paprika

⅛ teaspoon cayenne pepper

½ cup frozen or fresh peas

1 cup cooked lima beans

6 frozen artichoke hearts, cut in quarters

¼ pound snap peas or snow peas, strings removed

Wash the rice and place in a pot with 6 cups of the broth and the saffron. Bring to a boil, lower to a simmer, cover, and cook for 30 minutes.

Meanwhile, heat the oil in a paella pan measuring 17–18 inches at its widest point (or in a shallow casserole of a similar size), over 2 burners if necessary. Add the pine nuts and sauté over medium heat until lightly browned. Add the peppers and sauté until slightly softened.

Stir in the scallions and garlic, and cook 1 minute more. Raise the heat, add the tomatoes and parsley, and cook until the liquid from the tomatoes has cooked away. Stir in the paprika, cayenne, peas, lima beans, and artichokes.

Transfer the rice with its broth to the paella pan and mix well with the vegetables. Stir in the remaining 2 cups broth, bring to a boil, then simmer about 15 minutes, stirring and rotating the pan occasionally, until the rice is no longer soupy but a little liquid remains to continue cooking the rice. (There should be less liquid remaining than for other paellas since brown rice absorbs liquid more slowly.)

Preheat the oven to 350° F for a gas oven, 400° F for electric. Stir in the snap peas and transfer to the oven for about 25 minutes (it may need a few more minutes in an electric oven), until the rice is almost al dente. Remove to a warm spot, cover with foil, and let sit 10 minutes, until the rice is cooked to taste.

Vegetable Paella with Spicy Garlic Sauce

(Paella de Verduras con Salsa Picante de Ajo)

This all-vegetable paella—one of my favorites—incorporates twelve vegetables and is so full of flavor that you will never notice the absence of meat, poultry, or fish. A spicy sauce, made with many of the same ingredients used to make the rice, echoes the flavors of the rice, but it is bolder because the sauce is not cooked (the paella is also excellent without the sauce). Despite so many vegetables (you can of course add or omit vegetables as you choose), this paella is easy to prepare. Just be sure that everything is chopped and at hand before beginning the paella.

Serves 6 to 8

Spicy Garlic Sauce (page 210)

1 medium zucchini, cut in ½-inch crosswise slices and then each slice quartered

2 cups well washed, dried, and coarsely chopped spinach leaves

2 medium red bell peppers, finely chopped

4 teaspoons finely chopped fresh hot red or green pepper

6 frozen artichoke hearts, quartered

⅔ cup frozen lima beans

6 large shiitake or other mushrooms (about ½ pound), stems trimmed and coarsely chopped

½ cup frozen or fresh peas

8 medium scallions, trimmed and coarsely chopped

6 cups chicken broth, canned or homemade (page 207), or vegetable broth, canned or homemade (page 208)

¼ teaspoon crumbled thread saffron

8 tablespoons olive oil

1 medium tomato, skinned, seeded, and finely chopped

4 cloves garlic, minced

1 teaspoon sweet paprika, preferably Spanish smoked

1 teaspoon ground cumin

2 tablespoons minced parsley

3 cups imported Spanish or Arborio short-grain rice

Kosher or sea salt

½ pound snap peas or snow peas, strings removed

Make the spicy garlic sauce according to the instructions and transfer to a serving bowl.

Combine in a large bowl the zucchini, spinach, sweet and hot red peppers, artichokes, lima beans, mushrooms, peas, and scallions. Combine the broth and saffron in a pot and keep hot over the lowest heat.

Preheat the oven to 400° F for gas oven, 450° F for electric.

Heat the oil in a paella pan measuring 17–18 inches at its widest point (or in a shallow casserole of a similar size), over 2 burners if necessary. Add the vegetables from the bowl and sauté about 3 minutes over high heat, until the vegetables are slightly softened. Stir in the tomato, garlic, paprika, cumin, and parsley, and cook 2 minutes more. Add the rice and coat well with the pan mixture.

Pour in all the hot broth and bring to a boil. Taste for salt and continue to boil about 5 minutes, stirring and rotating the pan occasionally, until the rice is no longer soupy but sufficient liquid remains to continue cooking the rice. Stir in the snap peas and transfer to the oven. Cook, uncovered, 10–12 minutes in a gas oven, 15–20 minutes electric, until the rice is almost al dente. Remove to a warm spot, cover with foil, and let sit 5–10 minutes, until the rice is cooked to taste. Pass the garlic sauce separately.

Eggplant, Olive, Anchovy, and Caper Paella

(Paella de Berengena con Aceituna, Anchoa, y Alcaparras)

Except for a touch of anchovy, this is an all-vegetable paella. With the meatiness of the eggplant, the bite of the olives, anchovy, and capers, and a slight piquancy, this is without question a complete and splendid meal.

Serves 6

9 tablespoons olive oil

4 cloves garlic, mashed to a paste in a mortar or garlic press

2½ pounds small to medium eggplants, skin on and cut in ⅛-inch rounds

Kosher or sea salt

4 tablespoons minced parsley

8 cloves garlic, minced

6 cups chicken broth, canned or homemade (page 207), or vegetable broth, canned or homemade (page 208)

¼ teaspoon crumbled thread saffron

1 medium red bell pepper, finely chopped

1 medium green bell pepper, finely chopped

2 fresh red medium-hot chile peppers, such as arbol, finely chopped

1 small onion, finely chopped

2 medium scallions, trimmed and chopped

1 medium tomato, finely chopped

1 teaspoon sweet paprika, preferably Spanish smoked

10 medium-size cured black olives, such as calamata, pitted and cut in several pieces

8 anchovy fillets, chopped

½ teaspoon capers, whole if nonpareil, otherwise chopped

3 cups imported Spanish or Arborio short-grain rice

Combine in a small bowl 4 tablespoons of the oil with the mashed garlic. Sprinkle the eggplant slices well with salt and drain in a colander for 20–30 minutes.

Preheat the oven to 425° F.

Dry the eggplant slices well between paper towels. Grease a cookie sheet and arrange the eggplant in a single layer. Brush with the garlic and oil mixture, and bake for 10 minutes, turning once. Set aside about one-fourth of the eggplant for garnish and coarsely chop the rest.

In a mortar or miniprocessor, mash to a paste the parsley, minced garlic, and ¼ teaspoon salt. Combine the broth and saffron in a pot and keep hot over the lowest heat.

Lower the oven temperature to 400° F for gas oven, 450° F for electric.

Heat the remaining 5 tablespoons oil in a paella pan measuring 17–18 inches at its widest point (or in a shallow casserole of a similar size), over 2 burners if necessary. Sauté the red and green bell peppers, chile peppers, and onion over medium-high heat until the peppers are slightly softened. Add the scallions and tomato, and cook 2 minutes more. Stir in the paprika, olives, anchovy fillets, capers, and chopped eggplant. Mix in the rice and coat well with the pan mixture.

Pour in all the hot broth and bring to a boil. Taste for salt and continue boiling, stirring and rotating the pan occasionally, until the rice is no longer soupy but sufficient liquid remains to continue cooking the rice, about 5 minutes.

Arrange the eggplant slices over the rice and transfer to the oven. Cook, uncovered, until the rice is almost al dente, 10–12 minutes in a gas oven, 15–20 minutes electric. Remove to a warm spot, cover with foil, and let sit 5–10 minutes, until the rice is cooked to taste.

Potpourri of Mushrooms Paella
(Paella de Setas Variadas)

Richly flavorsome and accented by the singular taste of cured ham (which you can elimi-nate if you would like a totally vegetarian rice), this paella is completely satisfying as a main course and is among my favorites. Use as many different kinds of mushrooms as you wish, but if you choose portobellos, remove the dark spongy underside or it will discolor the rice.

Serves 6 to 8

¼ teaspoon crumbled thread saffron

4 tablespoons minced shallots

Kosher or sea salt

4 tablespoons minced parsley

4 cloves garlic, minced

6 cups chicken broth, canned or homemade (page 207), or vegetable broth, canned or homemade (page 208)

8 tablespoons olive oil

4 medium leeks, white part only, very well washed and finely chopped

2 medium onions, finely chopped

½ pound Spanish serrano ham or prosciutto, cut in ¼-inch-thick slices and then diced

2 medium tomatoes, skinned, seeded, and finely chopped

¾ cup dry white wine

1½ pounds mushroom (such as a mixture of shiitake, oyster, cepes, and boletus), brushed clean, stems trimmed, and very coarsely chopped

3 cups imported Spanish or Arborio short-grain rice

In a mortar or miniprocessor, mash to a paste the saffron, shallots, ¼ teaspoon salt, parsley, and garlic. Heat the broth in a large pot over the lowest heat.

Preheat the oven to 400° F for gas oven, 450° F for electric.

Heat the oil in a paella pan measuring 17–18 inches at its widest point (or in a shallow casserole of a similar size), over 2 burners if necessary. Sauté the leeks and onions over medium heat until softened. Add the ham, cook 1 minute, then add the tomatoes and cook 1–2 minutes more. Pour in the wine and boil away.

Add the mushrooms and cook 1–2 minutes to soften, then stir in the rice and coat well with the pan mixture. Pour in the hot broth and bring to a boil. Add the mortar mixture, taste for salt, and continue to boil, stirring and rotating the pan occasionally, until the rice is no longer soupy but sufficient liquid remains to continue cooking the rice, about 5 minutes.

Transfer to the oven and cook, uncovered, until the rice is almost al dente, 10–12 minutes in a gas oven, 15–20 minutes electric. Remove to a warm spot, cover with foil, and let sit 5–10 minutes, until the rice is cooked to taste.

TURRÓN:
SPANISH CANDY WITH A MOORISH PAST

Turrón, a Spanish almond nougat candy, has been a traditional sweet in the Valencia region since the fourteenth century. It appears on every Christmas table in Spain and is a fitting finale to a holiday meal. Because of its association with Christmas, *turrón* has remained a strictly seasonal sweet that you are not likely to find at other times of year (except at airport shops in Spain).

It was the Moors who planted almond trees and sugarcane in the Valencia region, then introduced Spain to *turrón.* Today *turrón* continues to be made locally in the small town of Jijona, hidden in the Peñarroja Mountains of Alicante and surrounded by almond trees. Here, all the essential ingredients for *turrón* are found: wonderfully sweet almonds, sugar, and wild honey made from orange blossoms and rosemary.

Turrón comes in two basic varieties: crackling Alicante style, made from toasted almonds, honey, sugar, and egg whites, and soft Jijona style, which pulverizes hard *turrón* and melds its ingredients into a slightly crumbly, caramel-colored paste. Chocolate *turrón* is fast becoming a favorite.

Turrón is typically cut into pieces and eaten on its own, but I also love it with ice cream. You can break up Alicante-style *turrón* and fold it into softened vanilla ice cream. Or try crumbling Jijona-style *turrón* over ice cream for an instant and uniquely Spanish dessert treat.

Green and Yellow Squash Paella with Pesto

(Paella de Calabaza con Puré de Basílico)

An extraordinary rice with a hauntingly nutty flavor that is a result of combining pesto and squash. The great taste of this paella is much more than the sum of its parts—it's the inter-action and blending of ingredients that create a taste that stays with you. This paella easily stands on its own as a main course.

Serves 4

3 cups chicken broth, canned or homemade (page 207), or vegetable broth, canned or homemade (page 208)

⅛ teaspoon crumbled thread saffron

4 tablespoons olive oil

2 tablespoons pine nuts

½ small onion, finely chopped

1 long, thin mildly hot green pepper, finely chopped (about 3 tablespoons)

½ green bell pepper, finely chopped

3 ounces oyster or other mushrooms, stems trimmed and coarsely chopped (about 1 cup)

1 cup washed, well-dried, chopped, and lightly packed spinach leaves

½ pound zucchini, cut in ½-inch crosswise slices and then quartered

½ pound yellow squash, cut in ½-inch crosswise slices and then quartered

Kosher or sea salt

3 tablespoons finely chopped tomato

¼ teaspoon sweet paprika, preferably Spanish smoked

1½ cups imported Spanish or Arborio short-grain rice

3 tablespoons Pesto Sauce (page 210)

Combine the broth and saffron in a pot and keep hot over the lowest heat.

Preheat the oven to 400° F for gas oven, 450° F for electric.

Heat the oil in a paella pan measuring 13 inches at its widest point (or in a shallow casserole of a similar size). Add the pine nuts and brown lightly over medium heat. Add the onion and the hot and bell peppers, and sauté until the vegetables are softened. Stir in the mushrooms, spinach, zucchini, and yellow squash, season with salt, and cook 2–3 minutes. Stir in the tomato and paprika.

Add the rice and coat well with the pan mixture. Pour in the broth and bring to a boil. Add the pesto sauce, taste for salt, and continue to boil, stirring occasionally, until the rice is no longer soupy but sufficient liquid remains to continue cooking the rice, about 5 minutes.

Transfer to the oven and cook, uncovered, 10–12 minutes in a gas oven, 15–20 minutes electric, until the rice is almost al dente. Remove to a warm spot, cover with foil, and let sit about 5 minutes, until the rice is cooked to taste.

Baked Rice with Garlic, Potatoes, and Chickpeas

(Arroz al Horno con "Perdiu")

Most of the cooking of this rice is done in the oven (thus its name). It is a rice that includes potatoes, sliced tomatoes, and chickpeas, and without the sausage it is a traditional Lenten dish in Spain. Villagers once took their rice casseroles to the local baker for cooking because, in times past, ovens were not common in home kitchens. And although an earthenware casserole is customary for this rice, a paella pan is sometimes substituted.

A whole head of garlic, called perdiu, *or partridge, is placed over the rice as the symbolic meat.*

Be sure to serve a few cloves of the roasted garlic with each portion so that its flesh can be mashed and blended with the rice for richer flavor.

Serves 6

1 large head garlic, with excess outer skin rubbed off

1⅔ cups canned chickpeas (reserve the liquid)

About 5½ cups broth, preferably a mixture of chicken and beef broths

¼ teaspoon crumbled thread saffron

½ pound black sausage (preferably Spanish *morcilla*, see Sources, page 215), chorizo, or any other sausage, cut diagonally in ½-inch slices

8 tablespoons olive oil

1 medium potato, peeled and cut in ¼-inch slices

2 medium tomatoes, cut in ½-inch slices

Kosher or sea salt

1 medium onion, finely chopped

1 medium green pepper, finely chopped

2 cloves garlic, minced

1 medium to large tomato, skinned, seeded, and finely chopped

2 tablespoons minced parsley

½ teaspoon sweet paprika, preferably Spanish smoked

3 cups imported Spanish or Arborio short-grain rice

Preheat the oven to 400° F for gas oven, 450° F for electric. Place the whole head of garlic in a baking dish and bake while preparing the rice.

Mash ⅔ cup of the chickpeas through a strainer or ricer into a saucepan. Combine the broth and about ½ cup of chickpea liquid to make 6 cups. Pour into the saucepan, stir in the saffron, and keep hot over the lowest heat.

Heat a 15-inch greased, shallow fireproof casserole. Add the sausage and brown lightly on both sides. Drain on paper towels, remove to a warm platter, and drain off any fat in the pan. Heat the oil and slowly fry the potatoes, turning once, until brown and cooked through, about 5 minutes. Drain the potatoes on paper towels and transfer to the warm platter.

Raise the heat, add the tomato slices, and sauté 1–2 minutes, turning once. Remove to the platter. Sprinkle the tomatoes and potatoes with salt to taste.

Add the onion, green pepper, and minced garlic to the pan and cook slowly until softened. Stir in the chopped tomato and parsley, and cook slowly for 5 minutes. Add the paprika, then stir in the rice, coating well with the pan mixture.

Pour in the hot broth and the remaining 1 cup chickpeas. Bring to a boil, taste for salt, and boil about 3 minutes to reduce the liquid—just enough so that the garnishes will sit on top. Remove the whole head of garlic from the oven and place in the center of the paella pan. Arrange the potatoes, tomatoes, and sausages attractively over the rice.

Bake about 15 minutes (it may need a few more minutes in an electric oven), until the rice is almost al dente. Remove to a warm spot, cover with foil, and let sit 5 minutes.

Tapas and First Courses

Garlic Shrimp Toast

Garlic Mushroom Toast

Anchovy Toast with Alioli

Salmon and Shrimp Toasts

Shrimp and Spinach Pastries

Chorizo Pastries

Cheese and Leek Pastries

Tuna and Watercress Salad "La Trainera"

Piquillo Pepper Salad with
Raisins and Pine Nuts

Cheese Pâté with Walnuts and Peppers

Smoked Salmon and Bean Salad

Gazpacho, Córdoba Style

Sautéed Asparagus in Almond and Cumin Sauce

Sautéed Mushrooms with Serrano Ham and Shrimp

Baked Vegetable Medley with Toasted Garlic

Tuna with Roasted Vegetables and Garlic Sauce

Grilled Shellfish with Tomato and Cumin Purée

Grilled Shrimp with Cilantro Dips

Shrimp with Cumin-Scented Zucchini Purée

Shrimp and Fish Balls

Scallops, Santiago Style

Clams in Herbed Garlic Sauce

Mussels Vinaigrette

Brochette of Marinated Monkfish

Marinated Mini Pork Skewers with
Grapes "Casa Ruperto"

In this chapter you will find easy-to-make tapas and first courses that can be prepared mostly or wholly in advance, so you can concentrate on preparing the paella. You may choose dishes that will blend or contrast with your paella ingredients, according to taste. Some of my most successful menus have been all seafood—very popular today with guests keeping tabs on their diets—but vegetable- or meat-based starters also work very well. If your paella is meat or poultry, however, I find a seafood or vegetable first course ideal. Cooling gazpacho is welcome with just about any paella.

Most first courses, instead of being presented on their own, can be served as part of a tapas selection. Eating tapas style is fun, and tapas go hand in hand with Spain's exuberant lifestyle. Late lunch and dinner hours in Spain allow plenty of time for the age-old custom of gathering with friends or business associates in bars and taverns (they proliferate in astonishing numbers in Spanish cities) for good conversation over a glass of wine, beer, or sherry, accompanied by what is often a mind-boggling array of hot and cold tapas.

Chilled dry *fino* or nutty *amontillado* sherry from Spain are meant for tapas, and it is thought that the custom of eating tapas resulted from the need to nibble on something when drinking these fortified wines. Among my favorite dry sherries are Fino La Ina, Fino Quinta, and Tío Pepe.

Amontillados are dry but not bone-dry like *finos*, and some excellent ones are Osborne Amontillado and Hartley and Gibson Amontillado.

Many first courses, as well as several paellas, call for Spanish cured ham as an ingredient. It is a product with which Spaniards have carried on a love affair for centuries. *Jamón ibérico,* top-of-the-line mountain-cured ham from Spain, comes from native, free-range Iberian pigs and is ham of a quality and flavor beyond compare. It will soon be available in America, but in the meantime look for *jamón serrano*, also a superb ham from Spain. Otherwise, prosciutto is the best substitute when a recipe calls for cured ham.

Keep in mind the outstanding cheeses from Spain that make ideal tapas. Especially noteworthy are Manchego sheep's milk cheese from La Mancha, Cabrales blue cheese from Asturias, and Tetilla cow's milk cheese from Galicia, among many others that are now imported to the United States.

Garlic Shrimp Toast

(Tostada de Gambas al Ajillo)

One of the pleasures of staying at the Palace Hotel in Madrid is taking a short stroll down Medinaceli street to the wildly popular Bar Cervantes—where even standing room is at a premium—to enjoy some of their memorable tapas, most served canapé style on bread or toast.

This is one that I always order: a simple sauté of shrimp, garlic, and a touch of hot red pepper that is placed on a slice of toast spread with garlic mayonnaise. It is in essence gambas al ajillo, one of Spain's most exceptional tapas, but by serving it on toast with alioli, it is transformed into a completely different tapa. To make the classic version, simply eliminate the bread and alioli, thinly slice the garlic, then cook as directed, and serve in a shallow earthenware casserole.

Makes 12

½ pound small to medium shrimp,
    shelled
Kosher or sea salt
2 tablespoons extra-virgin olive oil
2 cloves garlic, peeled and lightly
    crushed
One 1-inch piece dried red chile
    pepper or ¼ teaspoon crushed
    red pepper

12 slices bread, cut at an angle ¼ to
    ⅜ inch thick from a long,
    narrow loaf
2 tablespoons Alioli (page 211) or
    Mock Alioli (page 213)
2 tablespoons minced parsley

Sprinkle the shrimp all over with salt and let sit at room temperature for 10 minutes. In a fire-proof earthenware casserole or skillet, heat the oil with the garlic and chile over medium heat until the garlic begins to color. Press it with the back of a wooden spoon to extract its flavor. Add the shrimp and sauté very briefly until they are just done (if you cut one, it should be opaque all the way through). Remove from the heat and discard the garlic.

Toast the bread lightly, spread with *alioli*, and arrange the shrimp on the toast. Sprinkle with parsley and serve right away.

Garlic Mushroom Toast

(Tostada de Setas al Ajillo)

Another wonderful tapa from Bar Cervantes in Madrid. As simple as it is, the combined flavors of mushrooms, garlic, cured ham, and olive oil are extraordinary. Oyster mushrooms are ideal, but other mild-flavored mushrooms can be substituted.

Makes 12 to 16

5 tablespoons olive oil

2 cloves garlic, finely chopped

½ pound oyster or other mild-flavored mushrooms, brushed clean, stems trimmed, and very coarsely chopped

One 1-inch piece dried red chile pepper, seeds removed

2 tablespoons diced Spanish serrano ham or prosciutto, cut from a ⅛-inch-thick slice

Salt

Freshly ground pepper

12–16 slices bread, cut at an angle ¼ to ⅜ inch thick from a long, narrow loaf

Alioli (page 211), Mock Alioli (page 213), or mayonnaise

2 tablespoons minced parsley

Heat the oil in a skillet and add the garlic, mushrooms, chile pepper, ham, and salt and pepper to taste. Sauté over medium heat until the mushrooms have softened. Turn off the heat, cover, and let sit. Discard the chile pepper.

Lightly toast the bread slices and spread with *alioli*. Spoon the mushroom mixture on the bread and sprinkle with parsley.

Anchovy Toast with Alioli

(Tostada de Anchoa con Alioli)

A mild alioli coating the toasted bread is perfect to counteract the strong taste and saltiness of anchovies. Use jarred anchovies rather than tinned if possible; they are generally higher quality and much more succulent and flavorful.

Makes 12

12 slices bread, cut ¼ to
⅜ inch thick from a long,
narrow loaf
6 tablespoons Alioli (page 211) or
Mock Alioli (page 213), reducing
the garlic to 2 cloves

12 anchovy fillets, cut in
half crosswise, at room
temperature
3 tablespoons minced parsley

Toast the bread lightly, then spread about 1½ teaspoons of the *alioli* on each slice and place 2 pieces of anchovy on top. Place under the broiler until the *alioli* is hot and puffy but not brown. Sprinkle with parsley and serve.

Salmon and Shrimp Toasts

(Tostadas de Salmón y Gamba)

I loved this elegant tapa that I recently ate at El Cenador del Prado restaurant in Madrid. It combines smoked salmon and shrimp drizzled with a mustard, dill, and onion vinaigrette and served on crisp garlic toast.

Makes 12 to 14

2 cloves garlic, mashed to a paste in a mortar or garlic press
10 tablespoons extra-virgin olive oil
12–14 bread slices, cut ¼ to ⅜ inch thick from a long, narrow loaf
1½ tablespoons freshly squeezed lemon juice
½ teaspoon Dijon-style mustard

2 tablespoons minced parsley
2 tablespoons minced fresh dill
4 tablespoons minced Spanish or Vidalia onion
Salt
Freshly ground pepper
4–6 ounces thinly sliced smoked salmon
12–14 small cooked shrimp

Preheat the oven to 350° F.

In a small bowl combine the garlic with 6 tablespoons of the oil. Place the bread slices on a cookie tray and bake in the oven for about 5 minutes, turning once. The bread should be crusty but not brown. Brush with the garlic and oil mixture.

In another small bowl, whisk together the lemon juice, mustard, and the remaining 4 tablespoons oil. Stir in the parsley, dill, onion, and salt and pepper to taste.

Shortly before serving, arrange a slice of salmon on each piece of toast and top with a shrimp. Stir the dressing and spoon over the shrimp and salmon (about 1 teaspoon per piece of toast).

Shrimp and Spinach Pastries
(Bric de Gambas y Espinacas)

Bric is a kind of phyllo dough that has recently become popular in Spain to enclose a variety of savory fillings. Unlike phyllo appetizers, which are drenched in butter and baked, these are quickly fried and are remarkably light and crisp. Olive oil fries best, for it quickly "seals" the pastry, blocking absorption of oil. Three exceptional versions of bric pastries follow, all from El Faro, my favorite restaurant in the city of Cádiz.

Spinach and shrimp bound by a white sauce is the filling in this version of these outstanding appetizer rolls that are always extremely popular with my guests.

Makes 16

2 tablespoons butter	Freshly ground pepper
2 tablespoons olive oil	Cayenne pepper
6 tablespoons flour	¼ pound uncooked shrimp, finely
½ cup plus 2 tablespoons milk	chopped
4 tablespoons bottled clam	1 cup spinach, washed, very well
juice or Fish Broth	dried, and finely chopped
(page 208)	(about 2 ounces)
2 tablespoons dry white wine	8 sheets phyllo dough
Salt	Olive oil for frying

Heat the butter and oil in a medium skillet until the butter is melted. Add the flour and cook 3 minutes, stirring constantly. Gradually pour in the milk, clam juice, and wine, and season to taste with salt, pepper, and cayenne. Cook over medium-high heat, stirring constantly, until thick and smooth. Stir in the shrimp and spinach, and cook about 5 minutes more. Spread the mixture on a dinner plate to cool, then refrigerate for 1 hour.

Cut a sheet of phyllo dough in half lengthwise; while working with 1 piece, cover the rest with a damp towel. Place about 1 tablespoon of filling in the middle at one end of the half sheet. Fold in each side over the filling and roll. Seal the end with a few drops of water.

Pour the oil into a skillet to a depth of at least ½ inch (or, better still, use a deep fryer) and heat until the oil quickly browns a cube of bread. Fry the pastries, in several batches if necessary, until golden brown, turning once. Drain on paper towels. They can be kept warm in a 200° F oven for up to 30 minutes.

Chorizo Pastries

(Bric de Chorizo)

This is the simplest of appetizers. Chorizo sausage is so flavorful, it needs no other ingredient or seasoning and is exceptional when enclosed in a crisp pastry.

Makes 16

¾ pound mild or spicy chorizo
    sausage, skinned and finely
    chopped

8 sheets phyllo dough

Heat a lightly greased skillet, add the chorizo, and slowly sauté to release the oil. Drain on paper towels.

    Enclose in phyllo and fry as directed in the previous recipe.

Cheese and Leek Pastries

(Bric de Queso y Puerros)

This appetizer calls for a mild creamy cheese that is brought to life by sautéed leeks and pepper. Fry as quickly as possible so the cheese does not liquefy and seep out of the pastries.

Makes 16

2 tablespoons olive oil
½ cup leeks (mostly white portion),
    very well washed and minced
1 cup mild soft cheese, such as

Spanish Tetilla or imported
    Fontina, coarsely grated
Freshly ground pepper
8 sheets phyllo dough

Heat the oil in a small skillet and sauté the leeks slowly until softened. Transfer to a bowl and cool briefly. Add the cheese and pepper to taste, and mix well.

    Enclose in phyllo and fry as directed on page 159.

Tuna and Watercress Salad "La Trainera"

(Ensalada de Bonito y Berros "La Trainera")

Madrid, despite its landlocked location, is famed for having Spain's highest quality seafood, but La Trainera restaurant sets even higher standards with its impeccable produce. In this salad, made with either fresh bonito (light meat tuna), cooked and marinated, or good-quality canned tuna, the tuna is beautifully complemented by fresh watercress and a vinaigrette made with Spanish sherry vinegar.

Everything can be done in advance except spooning the dressing over the salad, since the watercress tends to wilt rapidly.

Serves 6

One 6-ounce can solid white meat tuna, preferably packed in oil, drained

SALAD DRESSING

½ cup plus 1 tablespoon extra-virgin olive oil

4½ teaspoons sherry vinegar or 2 tablespoons other wine vinegar

2 tablespoons minced watercress leaves

1 bunch watercress (about ¼ pound), thick stems trimmed

2 teaspoons wine vinegar
Salt
Freshly ground pepper

¼ teaspoon Dijon-style mustard

1 clove garlic, mashed to a paste in a mortar or garlic press

⅛ teaspoon sugar
Salt
Freshly ground pepper

1 small red onion, cut in thin rings or slivered

In a small bowl, coarsely flake the tuna, then stir in the vinegar and salt and pepper to taste. Let sit while preparing the salad dressing.

Whisk together all the salad dressing ingredients. Arrange the watercress on 6 salad plates and scatter on the tuna and onion. Spoon on the dressing and serve right away.

Piquillo Pepper Salad
with Raisins and Pine Nuts
(Ensalada de Piquillos con Uvas Pasas y Piñones)

Jarred Spanish piquillos *from the region of Navarra are the aristocrats of peppers, in a league of their own. Slender little red peppers that narrow to a slightly twisted peak (thus their name), they are fire-roasted, hand-peeled, mildly piquant, and usually packed without preservatives. Their flavor is so sublime that even Spain's four-star restaurants use them straight from the jar.*

Piquillo peppers are available in specialty food shops and by mail order (see Sources, page 215) and are well worth the extra effort to find them. Otherwise, make your own pimientos (see page 132) or select jarred pimientos that have a bright red color. Drain them, return to the jar, cover with olive oil, and let sit for several hours. Their flavor will greatly improve.

This salad combines pimientos with pine nuts and raisins—a beguiling and typically Spanish medley of flavors.

Serves 4 to 6

2 tablespoons raisins
One 12-ounce jar (or equivalent)
    pimientos, preferably *piquillo*
    peppers, cut in ½-inch strips
2 tablespoons pine nuts
2 cloves garlic, minced
4 tablespoons finest extra-virgin
    olive oil

Cayenne pepper to taste (use
    only if peppers are not
    piquillos)
Kosher or sea salt to taste (use
    only if peppers are not
    piquillos)
2 tablespoons minced parsley

Soak the raisins in warm water for about 10 minutes. Drain. Combine the raisins in a bowl with all the other ingredients except the parsley. To serve, arrange on individual dishes or on a platter and sprinkle with the parsley.

Cheese Pâté with Walnuts and Peppers

(Pastel de Queso con Nueces y Pimientos)

Start the preparation several hours in advance.

This appetizer is a delicious mixture of Spanish Cabrales blue cheese from Spain's northwestern region of Asturias and fresh goat cheese, enhanced by the addition of walnuts and green pepper. I have often enjoyed it at Chez Victor, a favorite Spanish restaurant in the historic university town of Salamanca, where chef Victor Salvador is in charge of the kitchen and his spirited wife, Marguerite, oversees the dining room.

When sliced, served over salad greens, and bathed in a watercress vinaigrette, this dish makes a lovely first course. If you prefer to serve it as a tapa, spread the cheese mixture on bread and drizzle with the vinaigrette. Do make an effort to find Cabrales cheese, distinctively Spanish and unlike any other blue cheese you may know.

Serves 4

¼ pound Cabrales or Gorgonzola
   cheese

¼ pound fresh goat cheese

VINAIGRETTE

2 tablespoons minced watercress
   leaves

4 tablespoons extra-virgin
   olive oil

4 teaspoons wine vinegar

Mixed young salad greens, such as
   mesclun

12 walnut halves, coarsely chopped

2 tablespoons green bell pepper,
   finely chopped

1 teaspoon minced shallots or
   2 teaspoons minced onion and
   ½ teaspoon minced garlic

Salt

Freshly ground pepper

In a bowl, mash together the Cabrales and goat cheese, then add the walnuts and green pepper. Shape into a 2-inch square, enclose in plastic wrap, and refrigerate several hours or overnight.

To make the vinaigrette, whisk together all the ingredients. To serve, arrange the salad greens on 4 salad plates. Unwrap the cheese and slice into 4 portions. Place a slice on each plate of greens and spoon the dressing over the greens and cheese.

Smoked Salmon and Bean Salad

(Ensalada de Salmón y Judías)

Large white beans, smoked salmon, and anchovies bathed in a vinaigrette make up this excellent first course or tapa. It is a recent creation of El Faro in Cádiz, a restaurant dedicated to fine Andalusian cooking (especially the extraordinary seafood of this Atlantic coast). Under the guidance of restaurateur extraordinario, *Gonzalo Córdoba, and his sons, José Manuel and Fernando Córdoba, who are both chefs, El Faro is also one of the region's foremost innovators.*

When served on a bed of mesclun lettuce, this salad makes a very pretty presentation.

Serves 6

¾ cup finest extra-virgin olive oil
4 tablespoons wine vinegar
2 tablespoons minced parsley
Salt
Freshly ground pepper
2 tablespoons minced onion
2 tablespoons finely chopped
  pimiento

2 cups canned large white beans,
  preferably lima grands, drained
  and rinsed
8 anchovy fillets, coarsely
  chopped
6 ounces smoked salmon, thinly
  sliced and cut in ¾-inch pieces
Mesclun lettuce

In a bowl, whisk together the oil, vinegar, parsley, and salt and pepper to taste. Stir in the onion and pimiento. With a rubber spatula, fold in the beans, anchovies, and salmon. Allow to sit a few minutes (or as long as overnight) for the flavors to blend.

Arrange the lettuce on salad plates, then spoon the bean mixture in the center.

Gazpacho, Córdoba Style

(Salmorejo)

Prepare several hours in advance.

Beautifully rosy red and slightly thicker than other gazpachos, this is Spain's celebrated "liquid salad" since it is made in Córdoba, a province in Andalucía that produces superb olive oils. Salmorejo, as the soup is called here, reduces gazpacho to its most basic elements, which means that all ingredients—especially the tomatoes and olive oil—must be first rate.

The chopped egg and cured ham are not merely a garnish, they add essential flavor to this gazpacho.

Serves 6

3 slices good-quality sandwich
   bread, crusts removed
2¾ pounds very ripe and
   flavorful tomatoes,
   chopped
1 small to medium bell pepper,
   chopped
3 cloves garlic, minced
½ teaspoon cumin
2½ teaspoons salt, or to taste
¼ teaspoon sugar

¼ cup finest extra-virgin
   olive oil plus extra for
   drizzling
1 tablespoon sherry wine vinegar
   or 1½ tablespoons other wine
   vinegars
6 tablespoons chopped hard-boiled
   egg
6 tablespoons diced Spanish
   serrano ham or prosciutto, cut
   from ¼-inch-thick slice

Soak the bread by holding it under running water and squeeze dry. Place all the ingredients except the egg and ham in a food processor and blend until finely chopped. Pass through a food mill or strainer (if using a strainer, press with the back of a wooden spoon to extract as much liquid from the remaining solid pieces as possible). Taste for salt, adding more if necessary until flavors are fully developed. Depending on the tomatoes, it may be necessary to thin with a little water. Chill well, at least several hours or overnight.

To serve, drizzle a little olive oil over each serving and sprinkle with the egg and ham.

Sautéed Asparagus in Almond and Cumin Sauce

(Espárragos al Comino)

It is not surprising that I found this recipe of Moorish origin at the Villa Turística de Bubión in the isolated Alpujarra mountains in the Andalusian province of Granada, for it was here in the fifteenth century that the Moors, fleeing their Christian conquerors, took refuge. To this day cooking styles and ingredients—and architectural styles as well—show a marked Moorish influence. The flavors of cumin and crushed almond in this sauce are subtle and haunting, one of the best complements to green asparagus that I have ever tasted.

You can prepare the sauce in advance, then cook and sauté the asparagus shortly before serving.

Serves 4 to 6

2 tablespoons olive oil
1 dried sweet red pepper (*ñora*; see Sources, page 215) or mild New Mexico style, cored and seeded, or 2 teaspoons sweet paprika, preferably Spanish smoked
2 cloves garlic, peeled
1 slice bread, cut ¼ inch thick from a long, narrow loaf

1½ tablespoons blanched slivered almonds
¾ teaspoon ground cumin, or to taste
2 teaspoons wine vinegar
Salt
½ pound medium-size green asparagus spears

Heat the oil in a skillet large enough to accommodate the asparagus. Sauté the red pepper, garlic, bread, and almonds over medium heat, turning once, until the pepper is softened and the garlic, bread, and almonds are lightly browned. Transfer the garlic, bread, and almonds to a mortar or miniprocessor, leaving the oil in the skillet. Chop the pepper finely and add to the mortar along with 1 teaspoon water (if using paprika, add here). Mash to a paste, then stir in the cumin, vinegar, 2 tablespoons water, and salt to taste. (The mixture should have the consistency of a thick sauce; add more water if necessary.)

Microwave or boil the asparagus in water to cover (4–5 minutes in the microwave, about 12 minutes if boiling). Drain. Reheat the oil in the skillet and sauté the asparagus over medium-high heat for 1–2 minutes. Add the mortar mixture, heat, then cover and let sit for several minutes before serving.

Sautéed Mushrooms with Serrano Ham and Shrimp

(Setas Salteadas con Jamón y Gambas)

Shrimp, mushrooms, cured ham, and garlic are made for one another, and when sautéed in olive oil make a wonderful first course that is extremely quick and simple to prepare.

Serves 4 to 6

½ pound medium shrimp, shelled
Kosher or sea salt
3 tablespoons olive oil
1 clove garlic, minced
½ pound mushrooms, preferably oyster mushrooms, stems trimmed, brushed clean, and coarsely chopped

2 tablespoons matchstick-size Spanish serrano ham or prosciutto, cut from a ⅛-inch-thick slice
2 tablespoons dry white wine
4 tablespoons minced parsley

Sprinkle the shrimp well with salt and let sit for 10 minutes at room temperature. Heat the oil in a skillet and sauté the garlic. Before it colors, add the mushrooms, season with salt, and cook over medium heat until the mushrooms are softened. Add the shrimp and ham, and cook 1 minute. Pour in the wine and cook until it evaporates. Add 2 tablespoons of the parsley and cook 1 minute more, until the shrimp are just cooked through.

Transfer to a serving platter or individual plates and arrange so that several of the shrimp are visible on top. Sprinkle with the remaining parsley and serve right away.

Baked Vegetable Medley with Toasted Garlic

(Verduras al Horno con Ajo)

Exceptionally good before a paella, this mix of green vegetables is given a decidedly Spanish flavor by the addition of olive oil, cured ham, and toasted garlic.

The green beans, limas, and asparagus are precooked separately since cooking times vary (the microwave does the job fastest and allows the vegetables to keep their bright colors). This way each vegetable continues to keep its separate identity when served.

Serves 6

3 cloves garlic, minced
3 tablespoons minced parsley
¼ teaspoon kosher or sea salt
4 tablespoons plus 2 teaspoons extra-virgin olive oil
3 cloves garlic, cut in thin slices
12 scallions (white part only), cut in 3-inch lengths
¾ pound cooked green beans, preferably broad green beans

¾ cup cooked baby lima beans
30 very thin cooked green asparagus spears
1 large pimiento, cut in ½-inch strips
3 thin slices Spanish serrano ham or prosciutto, cut in 1-by-1½-inch pieces

In a mortar or miniprocessor, mash to a paste the minced garlic, parsley, and salt. Stir in 3 tablespoons of the oil.

Heat another tablespoon of oil in a small skillet. Add the sliced garlic and cook over medium heat until well browned. Drain.

Preheat the oven to 500° F.

Arrange the raw scallions, cooked green beans, lima beans, and asparagus in a shallow casserole, keeping each vegetable separate from the others. Drizzle with the oil mixture, garnish with the pimiento, and scatter on the ham and toasted garlic. Bake for 5 minutes before serving.

Tuna with Roasted Vegetables and Garlic Sauce

(Atún con Escalivada al Ajo Aceite)

A delectable first course, as pretty to look at as it is a treat to eat. Based on the traditional Catalan roast vegetable dish called escalivada *that includes peppers, onions, and tomatoes, it is served with raw tuna and drizzled with a blend of olive oil and garlic. Naturally, your tuna needs to be perfectly fresh and your olive oil the finest extra-virgin.*

Serves 8

¾ cup extra-virgin olive oil

4 cloves garlic, mashed to a paste

3 tablespoons minced parsley

1½ tablespoons thyme leaves or
   ¾ teaspoon dried

Kosher or sea salt

Freshly ground pepper

1 pound very fresh tuna, cut on the
   bias in ⅛- to ¼-inch slices

2 green bell peppers

2 red bell peppers

4 medium tomatoes, cut in half
   crosswise

2 medium onions, peeled and cut in
   half crosswise

Ground cumin

About 3 tablespoons nonpareil
   capers

Combine the oil with the garlic, parsley, thyme, and salt and pepper to taste. Arrange the tuna slices on a dish and brush with some of the oil mixture, coating the fish lightly. Cover with foil and refrigerate for 1 hour.

Heat the oven to 525° F.

Place the green and red peppers, tomatoes, and onions in a roasting pan and bake 25–30 minutes, turning the peppers once. Let cool, then peel, core, and seed the peppers and cut into ½-inch strips. Chop the tomatoes finely, removing as much of the skin as possible. Sliver the onions (remove the outer layers if tough).

Spoon the tomatoes into the center of 8 small dishes. Sprinkle with salt, pepper, and cumin to taste. Crisscross the green peppers and then the red peppers over the tomatoes. Top with the slivered onions and sprinkle with more salt. Spoon the remaining oil mixture over the vegetables. Arrange the tuna slices around the vegetables and sprinkle the tuna with salt. Scatter capers on top of each dish.

Grilled Shellfish with Tomato and Cumin Purée

(Mariscos a la Parrilla con Puré de Tomate y Comino)

This dish comes by way of my good friend, chef Tomás Herranz of El Cenador del Prado, one of Madrid's finest restaurants. It is a fine first course before paella and is equally good served in tapas style using the tomato purée as a dip. The shellfish is at its best when cooked on a charcoal grill, giving it a special flavor that pairs beautifully with the taste of fresh tomato and cumin.

Serves 6 to 8

12–16 extra-large shrimp in
   their shells
½ pound large sea
   scallops

½ pound very small whole squid,
   cleaned
Olive oil for brushing
Kosher salt

TOMATO AND CUMIN PURÉE

1½ pounds very ripe sweet
   tomatoes, skinned, seeded, and
   very finely chopped
3 tablespoons extra-virgin olive oil
2 teaspoons ground cumin,
   or to taste, preferably freshly
   ground

4 cloves garlic, peeled and
   crushed to a paste in
   a mortar or garlic
   press
1 tablespoon red wine vinegar
Salt
Freshly ground pepper

Minced parsley for garnish

Brush the shrimp, scallops, and squid on all sides with oil. Sprinkle all over with salt and let sit at room temperature for 10 minutes.

Meanwhile, make the tomato and cumin purée, combining all the ingredients in a bowl.

Heat a charcoal grill or a lightly greased stovetop griddle until very hot. Arrange the shrimp and scallops on the grill and cook over high heat for about 3 minutes, turning once. Add the squid and continue cooking, turning once, about 2 minutes more (the squid will toughen if cooked longer). The shrimp and scallops should be cooked through at about the same time.

Divide the tomato purée among 6 to 8 dishes. Place the squid and scallops over the mixture, then arrange the shrimp attractively over the other shellfish. Sprinkle with parsley and serve right away.

Grilled Shrimp with Cilantro Dips

(Gambas a la Parrilla con Mojos de Cilantro)

There are few things tastier and more appealing than shrimp grilled in the Spanish style— in their shells and sprinkled with coarse salt—and served with a Canary Island dip (mojo) or, if you prefer, with Salmorreta Red Pepper Sauce. This is a superb addition to any selection of tapas you might serve before a meal, or it can just as well be presented as a first course.

Serves 4 to 6

¾ **pound extra-large shrimp in their shells, preferably with heads on**
Kosher or sea salt
Olive oil
Lemon juice

Spicy Cilantro and Green Pepper Dip (page 211), Cilantro Mayonnaise (page 213), and/or Salmorreta Red Pepper Sauce (page 209)

Sprinkle the shrimp all over with salt and drizzle with oil. Let sit for 10 minutes at room temperature. Coat a skillet or griddle lightly with oil and heat to the smoking point. Add the shrimp and cook very briefly, turning once, until just cooked through. Sprinkle with lemon juice and serve right away, accompanied by one or more dips.

Shrimp with Cumin-Scented Zucchini Purée

(Gambas con Salsa de Calabacín y Comino)

I think this blend of zucchini, cumin, and basil, served at room temperature with shrimp, is inspired and nothing less than I would expect from my friend and talented chef Tomás Herranz, who works his magic at the Cenador del Prado restaurant in Madrid. It is a fine example of how the simplest ingredients in the hands of a master chef can result in an exceptional dish.

If this dish is to be part of a tapas selection, serve the purée as a dip.

Serves 6 to 8

2 small to medium zucchini (about 1 pound), cut in ¼-inch crosswise slices and then quartered
2 onion slices
2 tablespoons minced basil leaves or 1 teaspoon dried
1½ teaspoons ground cumin
1½ cups chicken broth, canned or homemade (page 207)

Kosher or sea salt
Freshly ground pepper
1 teaspoon freshly squeezed lemon juice
1–1¼ pounds extra-large shrimp, shelled
Minced fresh basil or parsley for garnish

Combine in a saucepan the zucchini, onion, 1 tablespoon of the basil leaves (or ½ teaspoon dried), 1 teaspoon of the cumin, and the broth. Bring to a boil, then simmer for 10 minutes.

Transfer to a food processor and purée, seasoning with salt and pepper to taste. Add the lemon juice, the remaining tablespoon of basil (or ½ teaspoon dried), and the remaining ½ teaspoon cumin. Let cool to room temperature.

Meanwhile, sprinkle the shrimp all over with salt and let sit 10 minutes. Grill the shrimp over hot coals, on a stovetop griddle, or in a skillet lightly coated with oil. Cook very briefly, until the shrimp just turn opaque at the center. Let cool.

Divide the sauce among 6 to 8 plates and arrange the shrimp attractively over the sauce. Sprinkle with the basil and serve.

Shrimp and Fish Balls

(Albóndigas de Gambas y Rape)

Monkfish is combined here with shrimp, pine nuts, and cured ham to make tasty "meat-balls." They are served either with Spicy Cilantro and Green Pepper Dip (page 211) called mojo (typical of Spain's Canary Islands) or with Cilantro Mayonnaise (page 213), seasoned with cilantro, capers, garlic, and anchovies.

Serves 6

2 tablespoons bread crumbs
Dry white wine
½ pound monkfish or scrod
½ pound shrimp
2 cloves garlic, minced
4 teaspoons minced Spanish
    serrano ham or prosciutto
2 tablespoons minced parsley

2 tablespoons chopped pine nuts
1 egg
¾ teaspoon salt, or to taste
½ teaspoon freshly ground black
    pepper, or to taste
Minced cilantro for garnish
Cilantro dip (see headnote)

In a small bowl, soak the bread crumbs in 2 tablespoons of wine. Place the fish and shrimp in a food processor and pulse until the seafood is finely chopped. Transfer to a bowl and mix in the garlic, ham, parsley, pine nuts, egg, salt, pepper, and soaked bread crumbs. Shape into 1-inch balls.

    Pour wine into a sauté pan to a depth of ½ inch and bring to a boil. Drop the fish balls into the wine, cover, and simmer about 4 minutes, until the balls are just cooked but still juicy. Sprinkle with the cilantro and serve accompanied by a cilantro dip.

Scallops, Santiago Style

(Vieiras a la Compostelana)

In Spanish cooking, scallops Santiago-style (coquille Saint Jacques) may have the same name as their French counterpart, but the preparation is entirely different. It is one of my favorite ways to eat scallops—with cured ham, garlic, and onion, topped with oven-crisped bread crumbs, and essentially without any sauce. It is a popular dish in the city of Santiago de Compostela, a place of pilgrimage to the tomb of the apostle Saint James (Santiago in Spanish) since the Middle Ages.

Serves 4 to 6

1 pound bay scallops or sea
   scallops cut in half
Kosher or sea salt
5–6 tablespoons olive oil
½ cup minced onion
1 clove garlic, minced
Pinch of saffron
2 tablespoons diced Spanish
   serrano ham or prosciutto, cut
   from a ¼-inch-thick slice

1 tablespoon minced
   parsley
2 tablespoons dry white
   wine
¼ cup dried bread crumbs
¼ teaspoon sweet paprika
2 teaspoons freshly squeezed
   lemon juice

Sprinkle the scallops all over with salt. Heat 1 tablespoon of the oil in a skillet and sear the scallops (they should not be fully cooked). Remove to a warm platter. Add another tablespoon oil, the onion, garlic, saffron, ham, and parsley. Sauté for 1 minute, then cover and cook for 10 minutes over very low heat.

Add the wine and any juices the scallops have released, raise the heat, and boil away the liquid. Stir in the scallops and add salt to taste.

Preheat the oven to 450° F.

Divide the scallops among 4 to 6 greased scallop shells or small ramekins. In a small bowl, combine the bread crumbs, paprika, a little salt, and the lemon juice. Sprinkle over the scallops and drizzle each scallop shell with 2 teaspoons oil. Place the shells on a baking sheet and bake about 10 minutes, until the topping is golden.

Clams in Herbed Garlic Sauce

(Almejas en Salsa Verde de Hierbas)

A Spanish green sauce is essentially garlic, white wine, and parsley, and always irresistibly good with clams as a tapa. But here the addition of other herbs adds interesting flavor. The clams sauté right in the sauce, so they must be thoroughly cleansed in advance.

Serves 6

2 tablespoons olive oil
2 dozen very small littleneck clams,
    or 4 dozen cockles or Manila
    clams, thoroughly cleansed
    (page 10)
⅓ cup minced onion
4 cloves garlic, minced
One 1-inch piece dried red chile
    pepper or ¼ teaspoon crushed
    red pepper

½ cup dry white wine
4 tablespoons minced parsley
1½ teaspoons thyme leaves or
    ¼ teaspoon dried
1½ teaspoons chopped rosemary
    leaves or ¼ teaspoon dried
¼ teaspoon dried oregano
1 bay leaf
2 tablespoons freshly squeezed
    lemon juice

Heat the oil in a large skillet. Add the clams, onion, garlic, and chile pepper, and sauté until the onion has softened, stirring occasionally. Pour in the wine and boil until it boils away. Add 2 tablespoons of the parsley, the thyme, rosemary, oregano, bay leaf, lemon juice, and enough water so that the pan always has some liquid. Continue cooking until all the clams have opened, covering the pan if necessary. Remove those that open first to a warm platter and discard any that do not open. Transfer the clams and the sauce to a shallow casserole, preferably earthenware, and sprinkle with the remaining parsley. Serve with plenty of good crusty bread to mop up the sauce.

Mussels Vinaigrette

(Mejillones en Vinagreta)

Prepare one day in advance.

As simple as this tapa is (and so convenient since it is made the day before), it always proves to be a great favorite with guests. Prepare plenty—they go fast!

Makes 2 dozen

MARINADE

1 tablespoon minced parsley

1 tablespoon minced tomato

1 tablespoon minced pimiento

1 tablespoon minced onion

¼ teaspoon whole nonpareil capers
or larger capers chopped

Salt to taste

1½ tablespoons wine vinegar

¼ cup extra-virgin olive oil

⅛ teaspoon Dijon-style
mustard

~

2 dozen medium mussels, cleansed
as directed on page 10

¼ cup dry white wine

1 tablespoon finely chopped hard-
boiled egg

1 tablespoon minced parsley

In a bowl, whisk together the marinade ingredients.

Place the mussels and wine in a skillet, cover, and boil. Remove the mussels as they open. Reserve 2 teaspoons of the mussel liquid and add to the marinade. Separate the mussels from their shells and save half of each shell. Place the mussel meat in the marinade, cover, and refrigerate overnight.

Add the chopped egg to the marinade and return a mussel with some of the marinade to each shell. Sprinkle with parsley and arrange attractively on a serving platter.

Brochette of Marinated Monkfish

(Brocheta de Rape Adobado)

Start the preparation several hours in advance.

This typically Spanish fish marinade, which includes herbs, cumin, and garlic, is common all over Andalucía, and when the fish is fried after marinating, it goes by the name bien-mesabe *("it tastes good to me"). Here, the fish is cut in cubes and grilled on skewers with vegetables. With an* alioli *sauce on the side, this becomes a great tapa or first course.*

Serves 4 to 6

MARINADE

1 tablespoon extra-virgin
 olive oil

1 tablespoon wine vinegar

2 cloves garlic, mashed to a
 paste in a mortar or garlic
 press

A few threads saffron

½ teaspoon dried oregano

1½ teaspoons thyme leaves or
 ¼ teaspoon dried

¼ teaspoon paprika, preferably
 Spanish smoked

1 bay leaf, crumbled

¼ teaspoon crushed red pepper

¼ teaspoon ground cumin

Kosher or sea salt to taste

1 pound monkfish, tuna, shark, or
 swordfish steaks, cut in 1½-inch
 cubes

Eight 1½-inch square pieces red
 bell pepper

8 large scallions, trimmed and cut
 in 2-inch lengths

8 large mushroom caps,
 such as shiitake, brushed
 clean

Alioli (page 211) or Mock Alioli
 (page 213)

In a large bowl, combine the marinade ingredients and fold in the fish, coating well with the marinade. Cover and refrigerate for several hours.

Thread the fish onto 4 or more skewers, alternating with the red pepper, scallions, and mushrooms. Grill, preferably over charcoal (or on a greased stovetop griddle), until the fish and vegetables are done to taste. Serve accompanied by the *alioli*.

Marinated Mini Pork Skewers with Grapes "Casa Ruperto"

(Pincho Moruno con Uvas "Casa Ruperto")

These well-spiced pork kabobs come from one of my favorite tapa bars in Spain, Casa Ruperto in Sevilla. A modest establishment facing a small communal patio, this bar fills to overflowing at peak tapa hours, and owner Ruperto and his nephew, José Manuel, work at a furious pace to keep up with demand. Sevillanos know that their marinated grilled quail, spicy snails, grilled pringá sandwiches, made with marinated fresh pork and sausages, and these mini pork skewers are beyond compare.

Although Ruperto is an old friend, he stubbornly refused to reveal his secret recipe for the pork kabob marinade but finally relented last year. And although the ingredients are not particularly unusual, the blend of flavors has an air of mystery. The red grapes—a wonderful contrast in taste and texture—are an addition I enjoyed at the restaurant of the Culinary Institute of America in St. Helena, California, where the menu includes several dishes from Spain.

As a first course I like to serve two skewers per person on a bed of mesclun salad greens. As a tapa, one kabob suffices.

Serves 4 to 8

MARINADE

2 teaspoons dry *fino* sherry or dry white wine

2 tablespoons extra-virgin olive oil

½ teaspoon ground cumin

Freshly ground black pepper to taste

1½ teaspoons thyme leaves or ¼ teaspoon dried

1 clove, crushed

⅛ teaspoon ground nutmeg

1 bay leaf, crumbled

¼ teaspoon crushed red pepper

1 tablespoon minced parsley

1 teaspoon lemon juice

4 cloves garlic, peeled and lightly crushed

½ teaspoon sweet paprika, preferably Spanish smoked

Kosher or sea salt to taste

1 pound boneless pork loin or tenderloin, cut in 1-inch cubes

32 large red seedless grapes

Olive oil for grilling

In a bowl, combine the marinade ingredients. Fold in the pork and turn to coat well. Marinate at least 1 hour at room temperature or longer in the refrigerator.

Thread the pork onto 8 small skewers, about 8 inches long, alternating with the grapes (4 grapes per skewer). Grease a stovetop griddle with oil and heat to the smoking point (or grill over hot coals). Place the skewers on the griddle, lower the heat slightly, and cook, turning once, until well browned and just cooked through, about 5 minutes.

Desserts

Dessert Sauces
Raspberry Purée
Strawberry or Kiwi Purée

Gossamer Lemon Custard

Almond Milk Custard

Apple Flan Loaf with Caramelized Sugar Syrup

*Chocolate Flan with
Almond-Flavored Chocolate Sauce*

Almond Crisps

Raspberry Almond Crisp Sandwiches

Crispy Almond Tile Cookies

Almond Pine Nut Cookies

Almond Crisps with Frozen Yogurt and Honey

Peach Yogurt Torte

Red Wine Sangria Sorbet

White Wine Sangria Sorbet with Melon and Kiwi

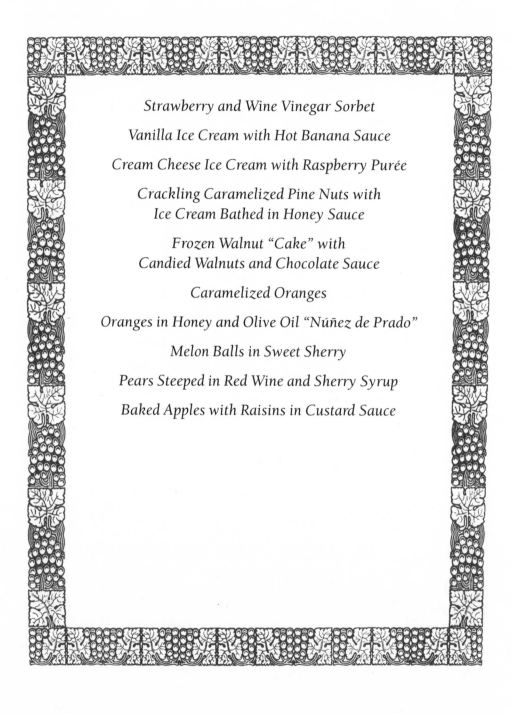

Strawberry and Wine Vinegar Sorbet

Vanilla Ice Cream with Hot Banana Sauce

Cream Cheese Ice Cream with Raspberry Purée

Crackling Caramelized Pine Nuts with
Ice Cream Bathed in Honey Sauce

Frozen Walnut "Cake" with
Candied Walnuts and Chocolate Sauce

Caramelized Oranges

Oranges in Honey and Olive Oil "Núñez de Prado"

Melon Balls in Sweet Sherry

Pears Steeped in Red Wine and Sherry Syrup

Baked Apples with Raisins in Custard Sauce

I have chosen uncomplicated, quickly prepared desserts for this chapter that are appropriate after a paella and, like the first courses, allow you to devote your time to preparing the paella. Desserts that are light, cool, and refreshing are the ones I find most appealing, and for that reason here are recipes for ice creams, custards, fruit desserts, and typically Spanish cookies.

Fruit has traditionally been the finish to a Spanish meal, but recently restaurants have increased their offerings to keep up with the times. Some of these recipes are included here. Nevertheless, centuries-old artless confections, many handed down from the Moors, continue to be inordinately satisfying.

Several desserts call for Spanish sweet sherry as an ingredient (you can read about dry aperitif sherries that are ideal with Spanish tapas in the Tapas and First Courses chapter), but keep in mind that Spanish sweet sherries such as *olorosos* (medium-sweet) and cream (very sweet) are exquisite as well to accompany any of the desserts in this chapter. Dry Sack and Almacenista are excellent *olorosos*, and Bristol Cream and Osborne Cream are tops in the cream category.

Dessert Sauces

Raspberry Purée

This simple purée and the one that follows are excellent with several of the desserts you will find in this chapter. Vary the amount of liqueur to taste or substitute water if you prefer.

Makes ½ cup

1⅓ cups raspberries, fresh or
    frozen
¼ cup sugar

1½ teaspoons fruit-flavored
    aquavit, Kirschwasser, orange
    liqueur, or water

Combine the raspberries, sugar, and liqueur in a food processor and blend until smooth. Strain.

Strawberry or Kiwi Purée

Makes ¾ cup

1½ cups cut and hulled
    strawberries or peeled kiwis
3 tablespoons sugar

Fruit-flavored aquavit,
    Kirschwasser, orange liqueur,
    and/or water

Combine the fruit and sugar in a food processor and beat until finely chopped. With the motor running gradually add enough liqueur and/or water to form a purée. Strain.

Gossamer Lemon Custard
(Delicia de Limón)

This ultralight lemon dessert is somewhat like the filling of a lemon pie but without any thickener except a small amount of egg—just enough to set the custard. It is served over a fruit purée (strawberry or kiwi) and garnished with fruit and a dollop of sweetened whipped cream to slightly cut the tartness. The recipe is adapted from the elegant Urepel restaurant in the beautiful seaside city of San Sebastián in northern Spain.

Serves 6

Butter to grease custard cups
¾ cup plus 3 tablespoons freshly
    squeezed strained lemon juice
1 cup sugar
¾ teaspoon grated lemon rind

3 eggs
Strawberry or Kiwi Purée (page 184)
Whipped cream, slightly sweetened
Whole or cut-up strawberries or
    sliced kiwi

Preheat the oven to 425° F.

Grease 6 custard cups well with butter. Using an electric beater, beat together the lemon juice, sugar, and lemon rind. Add the eggs one at a time and beat about 1 minute after each addition.

Pour into the custard cups and bake in a pan of hot water until just set, 15–20 minutes. Remove from the water and let cool.

To serve, spoon 2 tablespoons of the fruit purée on each of 6 dessert dishes. Unmold the custard over the purée, top with a dollop of whipped cream, and garnish with strawberries or kiwi.

Almond Milk Custard
(Mató Catalán)

Start the preparation four hours in advance.

This is a Catalán specialty, a soothing, satisfying dessert made with almonds and gelatin. The almonds are used only to flavor the milk, and the result is a wonderful pure white custard (it has no eggs) with the taste of almonds. Fresh fruit (strawberries are especially good) is an ideal accompaniment.

Serves 4

¼ pound slivered blanched almonds (about 1 cup)	1 cinnamon stick
	Peel of ½ lemon
⅓ cup sugar	1 envelope (¼ ounce) gelatin
1⅓ cups milk	Sliced or chopped fresh fruit

In a food processor, beat the almonds and sugar until the almonds are as finely ground as possible. With the motor running, gradually add ⅔ cup water. Transfer to a bowl, cover, and let rest in the refrigerator for about 4 hours. Strain, pressing with the back of a wooden spoon to extract as much liquid as possible from the almonds.

Heat 1 cup of the milk and the reserved almond liquid in a saucepan with the cinnamon stick and lemon peel. Simmer slowly about 15 minutes. Soften the gelatin in the remaining ⅓ cup milk and add to the saucepan. Simmer about 2 minutes more, until the gelatin is dissolved. Let cool.

Discard the cinnamon stick and lemon peel. Pour the almond milk into 4 custard cups. Refrigerate until the gelatin has set. Bring to room temperature before serving.

Loosen the edges of the custard with a knife and turn out onto 4 dessert dishes. Garnish with the fresh fruit.

Apple Flan Loaf with Caramelized Sugar Syrup

(Flan de Manzana con Azúcar Acaramelado)

This unusually delicate flan can be found in the lovely seaside city of San Sebastián in northern Spain at the exceptional Panier Fleuri restaurant, where María Jesús Fombellida presides. The restaurant is especially noted for its outstanding desserts.

Although this flan lacks milk (a characteristic ingredient of flan), puréed apples and eggs provide the body to set the custard. As the flan cooks in a loaf pan, it separates into two distinct layers—a more textured layer of apple purée and another of silky smooth custard. Sliced and bathed in caramelized sugar, it is one of the best flans I have ever eaten. Any kind of berry makes a pretty garnish and heightens the flavor.

Serves 5 to 6

1 pound Golden Delicious apples, peeled, cored, and cut in quarters, then cut in half	1 tablespoon freshly squeezed lemon juice
4 tablespoons sweet butter, cut in several pieces	2 tablespoons dry white wine
	⅛ teaspoon ground cinnamon
	⅛ teaspoon ground nutmeg

CARAMELIZED SUGAR SYRUP

½ cup sugar	8 tablespoons hot water
5 eggs	Fresh berries for garnish
½ cup sugar	(optional)

In a saucepan, combine the apples with the butter, lemon juice, wine, cinnamon, and nutmeg. Cover and simmer about 20 minutes, until the apples are tender.

Meanwhile, make the caramelized sugar syrup. In a small saucepan, dissolve the sugar in 3 tablespoons of the water. Cook over high heat, stirring constantly, until the mixture is syrupy and turns a light golden color. Turn off the heat. Slowly and very carefully stir in the remaining 5 tablespoons water. Pour into a loaf pan measuring 7½ by 3½ by 2 inches.

Preheat the oven to 350° F.

When the apples are done, uncover, turn up the flame, and cook until the liquid disappears. Pass through a strainer. In a bowl, whisk together the eggs and sugar, then whisk in the purée. Pour the mixture into the loaf pan, place the pan in another pan filled with water (*bainmarie*) and bake about 1 hour and 10 minutes, until the custard is fairly firm to the touch at the center. Let cool, chill well (it can be made a day in advance), then unmold onto a serving dish. Cut in ½-inch slices and place 2 slices on each dessert dish. Spoon on the caramelized sugar and garnish with berries if you wish.

Chocolate Flan with Almond-Flavored Chocolate Sauce

(Flan de Chocolate con Salsa de Chocolate al Sabor de Almendra)

Chocolate, brought to Europe from the New World by Spaniards, at first evoked little interest; the Aztec's bitter brew was not to European taste. But once sugar was added, chocolate was transformed into the sensation of Europe.

Chocolate is very popular in Spain as a candy (it is even put between slices of bread as an afternoon snack for children), but, curiously, it has never been a popular dessert ingredient. An exception is this chocolate flan—dark and rich, flavored with almond liqueur, bathed in chocolate syrup, and topped with whipped cream and almonds.

Makes 6

4 ounces dark unsweetened
   chocolate, cut in pieces
2 cups milk
⅛ teaspoon salt

CHOCOLATE SAUCE

2 ounces unsweetened dark
   chocolate
1 tablespoon butter
½ cup plus 2 tablespoons sugar

Whipped cream for garnish
   (optional)

2 whole eggs plus 2 yolks
½ cup sugar
4 tablespoons almond liqueur, such
   as Amaretto

Pinch of salt
2 tablespoons almond liqueur,
   such as Amaretto
¼ teaspoon almond extract

Sliced almond for garnish

To make the flan, place the chocolate in a small bowl and melt in a microwave oven. In a saucepan, heat the milk and salt, then stir in the melted chocolate and cook over medium heat, stirring frequently, until the chocolate is fully incorporated. Turn off the heat.

Preheat the oven to 350° F.

In a bowl, whisk together the eggs and sugar. Gradually stir in the chocolate milk mixture and the almond liqueur. Grease 6 custard cups and pour in the flan. Place the custard cups in a pan of hot water (*bainmarie*) and bake for 1 hour, or until set. Let cool.

Meanwhile, make the chocolate sauce. Melt the chocolate and butter together in a cup or small bowl in a microwave oven. In a saucepan, combine the sugar, salt, and ½ cup water. Whisk in the chocolate mixture and cook over medium heat, stirring constantly, until thickened (do not boil). Cool slightly, then stir in the almond liqueur and almond extract.

Spoon about 2 tablespoons chocolate sauce onto 6 dessert plates. Unmold the flan over the sauce and place a dollop of whipped cream on top, if you wish. Sprinkle with almonds.

Almond Crisps

(Crujientes de Almendra)

Among my very favorites, these delightfully crisp and richly almond-flavored cookies (made with only 2 tablespoons of flour) are splendid on their own or as a base for other desserts, such as Raspberry Almond Crisp Sandwiches (page 190) or Almond Crisps with Frozen Yogurt and Honey (page 192). They are extremely quick and easy to make.

Makes twelve 3½-inch cookies

⅔ cup (about 4 ounces) slivered
  blanched almonds
⅔ cup sugar
2 tablespoons flour

½ teaspoon grated lemon
  rind
⅛ teaspoon salt
6 tablespoons sweet butter

Preheat the oven to 350° F.

Place the almonds, sugar, flour, lemon rind, and salt in the bowl of a food processor and beat until the almonds are as finely chopped as possible. Add the butter and pulse until the butter is fully incorporated and the mixture holds together.

Form the dough into 1½-inch balls and place, well spaced, on a cookie sheet lined with greased foil. Flatten with your fingers into 2½-inch circles and bake about 10 minutes, until golden all over. Let cool slightly, then carefully remove from the foil with a metal spatula and transfer to a cooling rack.

Raspberry Almond Crisp Sandwiches

(Pastelillos de Frambuesa)

A most elegant dessert that looks and tastes far more sophisticated than its simple preparation suggests. Raspberries bound with whipped cream are sandwiched between two almond wafers and served over a pool of raspberry purée.

Serves 6

1 recipe Almond Crisps (page 189)
Recipe for Raspberry Purée
   (page 184), doubled
12 tablespoons whipped cream,
   sweetened to taste

¾ pound fresh raspberries or other
   berries
Confectioners' sugar
Raspberries or other berries for
   garnish

Make the almond crisps and raspberry purée as directed. Spread 1 tablespoon of the whipped cream over 1 of the cookies. Arrange about 25 raspberries over the whipped cream, spread a second cookie with another tablespoon whipped cream, and place over the raspberries. Repeat for the remaining 5 sandwiches.

    Spoon 2 tablespoons raspberry purée on each of 6 dessert plates. Place a raspberry sandwich on top of the sauce, dust with confectioners' sugar, and garnish with 1 or more raspberries at the center of the cookie.

Crispy Almond Tile Cookies

(Tejas de Almendra)

Teja literally means a curved roof tile, which these crisp, delicate, and totally irresistible cookies resemble. They have become a fashionable finale to a meal in many of Spain's elegant restaurants, either as individual cookies or as one oversized cookie shared by all. They are delightful on their own or as accompaniments to custard, ice cream, or fruit desserts.

Makes about 16

6 tablespoons sweet butter, softened	3 unbeaten egg whites
1¼ cups confectioners' sugar	½ cup flour
	Sliced almonds

Place the butter and sugar in a bowl and beat together with a wooden spoon. Add the egg whites one at a time and mix well after each addition. Stir in the flour and continue to mix until the batter is smooth and about the consistency of a thick béchamel sauce.

Preheat the oven to 325° F.

Line a cookie sheet with foil and grease the foil well with butter (you will have to make the cookies in several batches). Drop the batter, well spaced, by level tablespoons, and, using a rubber spatula, spread with a swirling motion into thin circles about 3 inches across. Sprinkle well with sliced almonds. Bake for 12–15 minutes, until the edges are brown and the centers are firm. Let cool a few seconds, then carefully lift 1 cookie at a time with a metal spatula and place, bottom down, over a rolling pin. Press the cookie close to the rolling pin to give it a good shape. Remove and let cool. Repeat for the remaining cookies. (If the cookies become too crisp to shape, return them to the oven for a minute to soften.)

Almond Pine Nut Cookies

(Pastas de Piñones)

I have always loved these soft chewy cookies, made with ground almonds instead of flour and studded with pine nuts. When I am in Madrid, I invariably pay a visit to El Riojano bakery just off the Puerta del Sol to buy a box. My goal is to take them home, but they rarely last that long.

Makes 1 dozen

4 tablespoons pine nuts	1 teaspoon anisette or other sweet liqueur
¼ pound (about 1 cup) slivered blanched almonds	¼ teaspoon ground cinnamon
½ cup sugar	½ teaspoon grated lemon rind
1 egg white	

Preheat the oven to 350° F.

Brown the pine nuts on a cookie tray in the oven for about 5 minutes (watch carefully). Remove from the oven and lower the temperature to 325° F.

In a food processor, grind the almonds with the sugar until as fine as possible. Add the egg white, anisette, cinnamon, and lemon rind, and pulse until fully incorporated. Shape the dough into 1-inch balls and place, well spaced, on cookie sheet lined with greased foil. Press with your fingers into 2-inch rounds, then lightly press some pine nuts into the cookies. Bake until lightly colored, about 10 minutes.

Almond Crisps with Frozen Yogurt and Honey

(Crujiente de Almendra con Helado de Yogur y Miel)

Once you have made the almond crisps, the rest is merely a matter of assembly. The result is a dessert in which the ingredients blend beautifully to create a cooling and very special finish to a meal.

Serves 6

½ recipe Almond Crisps (page 189)
1 pint best-quality frozen vanilla
   yogurt

6 tablespoons honey
Mint leaves (optional)

Make the almond crisps according to instructions and place one on each of 6 dessert plates. Top each with a large scoop of frozen yogurt and drizzle with the honey. Garnish with the mint leaves if you wish.

Peach Yogurt Torte

(Tarta de Yogur y Melocotón)

Quick and easy to make, this torte, topped with peaches and glazed with apricot preserves, is made with yogurt instead of milk and olive oil rather than butter. Olive oil is, in fact, excellent for baking, producing an unusually moist cake. But be sure to use only a mild-flavored oil—certainly not an extra-virgin oil.

Makes one 8½-inch torte

1 cup flour
2 teaspoons baking powder
⅛ teaspoon salt
1 egg
½ cup plus 2 tablespoons sugar
¼ cup lemon or vanilla yogurt
3 tablespoons pure olive oil
¼ teaspoon almond extract

2 ripe peaches, cut in ½-inch wedges
1 teaspoon freshly squeezed lemon juice
¼ teaspoon ground cinnamon
¼ teaspoon ground nutmeg
2 tablespoons apricot preserves
1 tablespoon sliced almonds
Whipped cream

Preheat the oven to 350° F.

Sift together the flour, baking powder, and salt. In a bowl, beat the egg with an electric beater until frothy, then gradually beat in ½ cup of the sugar. Continue beating until light and lemon-colored. Beat in the yogurt, oil, and almond extract, then gradually beat in the flour mixture.

Pour into a well-greased and floured 8½-inch springform pan. Arrange the peaches in slightly overlapping rows over the batter. Sprinkle with the remaining 2 tablespoons sugar, the lemon juice, cinnamon, and nutmeg.

Bake for about 1 hour, or until a toothpick inserted in the cake comes out clean. Cool and remove the springform. Heat the apricot preserves, then brush over the torte. Sprinkle with the almonds and serve with a dollop of whipped cream.

Red Wine Sangria Sorbet

(Sorbete de Sangría)

The following sorbets are based on typically Spanish ingredients. If they are frozen in an ice cream machine—the method I prefer—the results are smooth and creamy; if simply frozen in a freezer tray, the sorbet will be much more granulated.

Your guests may not be able to pinpoint the flavor of this singular sorbet as sangria, the original wine cooler from Spain, but they will surely appreciate and enjoy its fine taste. Uncommonly refreshing and slightly tart, this sorbet combines typical sangria ingredients— wine, sugar, citric juices, and, in this case, peach pulp—into a frozen palate-clearing finish to any meal.

Serves 4

½ cup sugar
Peel of 1 lemon, cut in several
  strips
Peel of 1 orange, cut in several
  strips
1 cinnamon stick
¼ cup freshly squeezed lemon
  juice

½ cup orange juice, preferably
  freshly squeezed
¾ cup dry red wine
2 tablespoons orange liqueur
1 ripe peach, peeled, pitted, and
  chopped

In a saucepan, combine the sugar, lemon and orange peels, cinnamon stick, and ¾ cup water. Bring to a boil, then simmer 20 minutes. Let cool, then chill. Discard the lemon and orange rinds. Combine the syrup with the lemon juice and orange juice, wine, and liqueur.

In a food processor, chop the peach as fine as possible. With the motor running, gradually add as much of the wine mixture as needed to make a purée, then mix in the rest. Freeze in an ice cream machine or in a freezer tray.

White Sangria Sorbet with Melon and Kiwi

(Sorbete de Sangría Blanca con Melón y Kiwi)

The melon and kiwi added to this white wine sorbet give a pronounced fruit flavor and turn the sorbet to pure white, except for flecks of the kiwi's black seeds. It is excellent paired with Strawberry and Wine Vinegar Sorbet (see below), which offers a superb contrast of taste and color.

Serves 6

1 cup sugar
Peel of 1 lemon, cut in several strips
2 kiwis, peeled and coarsely chopped
Two 1½-inch wedges honeydew
  melon or other light-fleshed
  melon, peeled, seeded, and
  chopped

½ cup freshly squeezed lemon
  juice
¼ cup orange liqueur
1½ cups dry white wine
Sliced kiwi for garnish

In a saucepan, combine the sugar, lemon peel, and 1½ cups water. Bring to a boil, then simmer 20 minutes. Let cool and chill. Discard the lemon peel.

Meanwhile, in a food processor, beat together the kiwis and melon. Gradually add the lemon juice and liqueur to make a purée. Mix in the wine and the reserved sugar syrup. Freeze in an ice cream machine or freezer tray. Serve garnished with kiwi slices.

Strawberry and Wine Vinegar Sorbet

(Sorbete de Fresa y Vinagre)

A sorbet with a brilliant strawberry color and intense fruit flavor. It is based on a simple Spanish dessert of strawberries prepared with sugar and vinegar.

Serves 6

¾ cup sugar

Peel of 1 lemon, cut in several
  pieces

2¼ pounds hulled strawberries
  (about 3 pints)

3 tablespoons lemon juice

3 tablespoons red wine vinegar

6 tablespoons fruit-flavored
  aquavit, Kirschwasser, or other
  fruit liqueur

Strawberries for garnish

To make the sugar syrup, combine in a saucepan the sugar, lemon peel, and 3 cups water. Bring to a boil, then simmer 20 minutes. Let cool, discard the lemon peel, and then chill.

Put the strawberries in a food processor with the lemon juice, vinegar, and liqueur, and purée. Strain. Combine the purée with the chilled syrup, and freeze in an ice cream machine or freezer tray. Serve garnished with strawberries.

Vanilla Ice Cream with Hot Banana Sauce

(Helado de Vainilla con Salsa Caliente de Plátano)

A quick-cooking banana topping for ice cream from the Canary Islands, Spain's paradisiacal islands off the coast of North Africa and the only part of Spain with the subtropical conditions necessary to grow bananas. The brown sugar sauce, flavored with lemon rind, nutmeg, and cinnamon, is flamed with orujo, *a Spanish liqueur made from grape skins that is similar to aquavit or Italian* grappa.

Serves 4

4 tablespoons butter

3 bananas, cut in ½-inch slices

2 tablespoons brown sugar

¼ teaspoon ground cinnamon

¼ teaspoon grated lemon rind

¼ teaspoon grated nutmeg

2 tablespoons *orujo, grappa,* or
  other liqueur

4 tablespoons sliced almonds

1 pint good-quality vanilla ice
  cream

Melt the butter in a medium skillet, add the banana slices, and sprinkle with the sugar, cinnamon, lemon rind, and nutmeg. Simmer about 2 minutes, turning the bananas occasionally with a rubber spatula.

Pour on the liqueur and flame. When the flame dies, spoon the sauce over the ice cream, sprinkle with the almonds, and serve immediately.

Cream Cheese Ice Cream with Raspberry Purée

(Helado de Queso con Salsa de Frambuesa)

You may choose to make your own cream cheese ice cream, but if you use a fine quality vanilla ice cream, this method is a quick alternative. A splendid ending to a meal.

Serves 4

3 ounces cream cheese, softened
1 pint vanilla ice cream,
   softened
Raspberry Purée (page 184)

Fresh raspberries or small
   strawberries
Mint leaves for garnish
   (optional)

In a bowl, beat the cream cheese with an electric beater until smooth. Beat in the ice cream, then refreeze, stirring occasionally. Prepare the raspberry purée.

Spoon 2 tablespoons of the purée on 4 individual dessert dishes. Top with a scoop of ice cream and scatter on the fresh raspberries. Garnish with mint leaves if desired.

Crackling Caramelized Pine Nuts with Ice Cream Bathed in Honey Sauce

(Helado de Piñones Garapiñados en Salsa de Miel)

Sugar- or honey-coated candied nuts have been a staple of Spanish sweets since time immemorial, and like most Spanish desserts of nuts, honey, and sugar, are of clear Moorish origin. To this day in most Spanish towns and cities you will find street vendors with push-carts offering these nuts as well as other nuts and candies. They often station themselves along shady promenades to entice Spaniards out for their daily stroll.

Although these candied nuts are usually made with almonds, pine nuts are excellent as well and much more delicate in size and flavor. Here I have sprinkled these crunchy nuts over ice cream and added honey sauce; the result is an appealing and refreshing dessert. Instead of scattering the nuts over the ice cream, you can soften the ice cream and fold in the nuts. They will remain crunchy for a couple of days.

Serves 4

Butter
½ cup pine nuts

HONEY SAUCE

½ cup honey
2 teaspoons warm water

½ cup sugar
¼ teaspoon ground cinnamon

½ teaspoon ground cinnamon

~

1 pint finest quality vanilla ice cream

Line a cookie sheet with foil and grease the foil well with butter. Combine in a skillet the pine nuts, sugar, cinnamon, and ½ cup water. Bring to a boil and boil over the highest heat, stirring constantly, until the sugar turns a dark golden color, about 5 minutes. Pour onto the prepared cookie sheet, spreading with a rubber spatula into a thin layer. Let cool completely. Peel off the foil and break or lightly pound the candied nuts into small pieces.

To make the honey sauce, combine the honey, water, and cinnamon in a small bowl. Spoon onto 4 individual dessert dishes, top with a scoop of ice cream, and sprinkle with the caramelized nuts.

Frozen Walnut "Cake" with Candied Walnuts and Chocolate Sauce

(Biscuit de Nueces con Nueces Garapiñadas y Salsa de Chocolate)

Prepare one day in advance.

In truth, this is not a cake at all but an ice cream given the appearance of a cake (it is made in a loaf pan) and given a slightly cakelike texture by the addition of ground nuts and beaten egg whites. It is served with a chocolate sauce and candied walnuts. If you are pressed for time, plain walnuts are also good. If you prefer not to use raw egg whites, an egg substitute made with egg whites works fine.

Serves 8 to 10

Butter
1 cup walnuts
5 tablespoons sugar
6 egg whites or 1 cup egg substitute made with egg whites
Pinch of salt
¾ cup heavy cream

¼ teaspoon vanilla extract
Chocolate Sauce (page 188)
Candied walnuts, made as for caramelized pine nuts (page 198), substituting ¾ cup coarsely chopped walnuts

Grease a loaf pan measuring 9¼ by 5¼ by 2¾ inches. In a food processor, beat the walnuts with 2 tablespoons of the sugar until the nuts are finely ground. Set aside. With an electric mixer, beat the egg whites until foamy, then beat in the remaining 3 tablespoons sugar and the salt. Beat until stiff but not dry (or until very thick, if using egg substitute).

In a separate bowl, whip the cream and vanilla extract until the cream is stiff, then fold in the egg white mixture and ground walnuts. Pour into the greased loaf pan, cover with foil and freeze overnight.

Make the chocolate sauce and the candied walnuts as directed.

To serve, place the bottom of the loaf pan in hot water and turn out onto a serving dish. Slice and place on dessert dishes, bathe in chocolate, and sprinkle with the candied walnuts.

Caramelized Oranges

(Naranjas en Azúcar Acaramelado)

What a pleasant sensation biting into this caramelized sugar glaze and finding a sweet orange underneath that suddenly explodes with juice. The coating, by the way, will stay hard for several hours, so these oranges can be prepared earlier in the day.

You may serve the oranges on their own, but they are also excellent served over a raspberry purée or with a plain pound cake or orange cake.

Serves 4

2 large oranges, peeled and all
   white pith removed
1 cup sugar
2 teaspoons vinegar
3 tablespoons orange liqueur

Raspberry Purée (page 184)
   (optional)
Mint leaves and fresh
   raspberries for garnish
   (optional)

Divide the oranges into segments, keeping the membrane intact. Dry on paper towels.

In a saucepan, combine the sugar, vinegar, and 2 tablespoons water. Bring to a boil and continue to boil, stirring constantly, until lightly caramelized, about 4 minutes. Slowly and carefully stir in the orange liqueur.

Working quickly before the sugar hardens (it can be liquefied by reheating), dip the orange segments in the caramelized sugar (keep fingers away since the syrup is very hot), and with the aid of a wooden spoon, coat on all sides. Place upright on a wire rack to dry.

If serving with raspberry purée, spoon 2 tablespoons of the purée onto each of 4 dessert dishes. Arrange the orange segments attractively over the sauce. Garnish with mint leaves and fresh raspberries if you wish.

Oranges in Honey and Olive Oil "Núñez de Prado"

(Naranjas con Miel y Aceite de Oliva "Núñez de Prado")

After a recent tour of the Núñez de Prado olive oil estate in the Cordoban city of Baena with a group of Americans we had taken there, we were treated to a delightful meal, which ended with these sliced oranges, bathed in a blend of honey and the Núñez de Prado family's finest extra-virgin unfiltered olive oil. Although the combination seemed unlikely, these oranges were most definitely a highlight of the afternoon. The oil cut the sweetness of the honey while contributing its own subtly fruity flavors.

The Núñez de Prado brothers, with Paco at the helm, produce one of the world's finest olive oils, but their methods are a step back in time. Theirs is an operation so simple—you might even say primitive—that it is hard to believe Núñez de Prado runs an international operation. Their olives are organically raised—no pesticides or chemical fertilizers— handpicked, washed with water, crushed by huge stones (as in Roman times), and then allowed to drip without pressure to extract the flor (flower) of the oil. It is stored underground, then poured into their distinctive bottles, hand-sealed with red wax, and numbered.

Serves 6

6 navel oranges

2 tablespoons honey

1½ cups sugar

2 tablespoons orange juice

2 tablespoons finest extra-virgin olive oil, ideally Núñez de Prado

2 tablespoons orange liqueur

Remove a thin peel from 2 oranges and cut in very fine julienne strips. Clean the pith from all the oranges, removing as much as possible. Place the julienne strips in a small saucepan with water barely to cover. Bring to a boil and simmer 10 minutes. Drain and run under cold water.

In a saucepan, bring to a boil the honey, sugar, orange juice, and ½ cup water. Boil slowly until the liquid is syrupy, about 10 minutes (230° F on a candy thermometer). Add the orange julienne strips and turn off the heat. When cool, stir in the oil and liqueur.

Slice the oranges and arrange in a large shallow bowl. Pour on the syrup and let sit at room temperature for 1 hour or more. To serve, divide the orange slices among 4 dessert dishes and spoon the sauce and orange julienne strips over them.

Melon Balls in Sweet Sherry

(Melón al Jerez Dulce)

An utterly simple and most refreshing dessert with the distinctive Spanish touch of cream sherry. Melon works particularly well, but other fruits would also be suitable. If you like, serve with a cookie, such as Almond Pine Nut Cookies (page 191) or Crispy Almond Tile Cookies (page 190).

Serves 4

¼ cup Spanish cream sherry or
    sweet red wine
½ cup cranberry or orange juice
1 teaspoon freshly squeezed lemon
    juice
1 tablespoon sugar
¼ teaspoon grated lemon rind

1 tablespoon chopped mint leaves
    or ½ teaspoon dried
¼ teaspoon mace
1 ripe and flavorful orange melon,
    such as cantaloupe or Cranshaw,
    cut with a melon scoop into
    balls

In a bowl, combine all the ingredients except the melon. Fold in the melon balls, cover, and refrigerate about 30 minutes, stirring occasionally.

Pears Steeped in Red Wine
and Sherry Syrup

(Peras en Jarabe de Vino y Jerez)

Prepare one day in advance.

For this easy-to-prepare fruit dessert, pears are simmered in red wine, and after the addition of sweet cream sherry and more spice, boiled down to a syrup. The pears steep overnight, absorbing all the subtle and appealing flavors of the syrup.

Serves 4

4 medium to large ripe but firm
    pears, peeled
Lemon juice
3 cups dry red wine
½ cup sugar
2 cinnamon sticks, cut in half

Two ¼-inch lemon slices, cut in half
¼ cup Spanish cream sherry or
    sweet red wine
¼ teaspoon mace
1 tablespoon honey, or to taste
Whipped cream (optional)

Rub the peeled pears all over with lemon juice. In a deep nonreactive saucepan in which the pears will fit fairly closely, combine the wine, sugar, cinnamon, lemon slices, and 2 cups water. Bring to a boil, then lower the heat and add the pears. Cover and cook at a high simmer for about 20 minutes, until the pears are tender. Remove the pears and set aside.

Add the sherry and mace to the wine mixture and boil down until syrupy (you should have about 1½ cups). Stir in the honey and return the pears to the syrup. Let sit at room temperature overnight, turning the pears occasionally in the syrup.

To serve, slice the pears in quarters and remove the core. Cut into wedges ¼ to ½ inch and arrange in overlapping rows on 4 dessert dishes. Spoon on the syrup and garnish with the cinnamon sticks and lemon slices. Place a dollop of whipped cream, if you wish, at the center.

Baked Apples with Raisins in Custard Sauce

(Manzanas Asadas con Uvas Pasas a la Crema)

Although still a very simple dessert, these baked apples take on added interest by the addition of raisins, almonds, sweet sherry, and a soft custard sauce. Both the apples and the custard can be made in advance and assembled when ready to serve.

Serves 6

3 large apples suitable for baking, such as McIntosh or Golden Delicious, peeled, cut in half lengthwise, and cored
Lemon juice
2 cinnamon sticks, each cut in 3 pieces

2 tablespoons sugar
2 tablespoons honey
2 tablespoons sweet sherry or other sweet wine
3 tablespoons raisins
Peel of ½ lemon, cut in several pieces

CUSTARD SAUCE

2 eggs, lightly beaten
¼ cup sugar
⅛ teaspoon salt

2 cups hot milk
½ teaspoon vanilla extract

～

6 large strawberries, preferably with their leaves (otherwise use mint leaves)

Sliced almonds for garnish

Preheat the oven to 350° F.

Rub the apple halves all over with lemon juice. In a shallow baking dish in which the apples will comfortably fit, combine the cinnamon sticks, sugar, honey, sherry, raisins, and lemon peel. Stir in 4 tablespoons water.

Arrange the apples in the baking dish, cored side up. Cover and bake, basting occasionally, for about 40 minutes, until the apples are just tender (do not overcook). Let cool.

Meanwhile, make the custard sauce. Combine in a heavy saucepan the eggs, sugar, and salt. Gradually stir in the hot milk and cook in a double boiler or over a pan of water (the water should not boil), stirring constantly, until the custard coats a spoon. Add the vanilla extract and let cool.

Remove the apples, cinnamon sticks, and raisins to another dish. Discard the lemon peel. Combine the syrup that remains in the baking dish with the custard. Spoon about 3 tablespoons on each of 6 dessert dishes and place an apple half, cored side up, over the custard. Fill the hollow of the apple with a strawberry. Scatter the raisins around the custard and garnish each plate with a piece of cinnamon stick. Sprinkle with the almonds and serve warm or at room temperature.

Broths, Sauces, and Dips

Chicken Broth

Fish Broth

Vegetable Broth

Garlic Sauce

Salmorreta Red Pepper Sauce

Spicy Garlic Sauce

Pesto Sauce

Spicy Cilantro and Green Pepper Dip

Alioli

Potato Alioli

Mock Alioli

Cilantro Mayonnaise

MAKING COMMERCIAL BROTHS BETTER

Canned chicken and vegetable broths and bottled clam juice are quite acceptable to use in a paella, but, of course, homemade broths will have much more flavor. If you don't have the time or the inclination to make broth from scratch, I suggest enhancing and enriching store-bought products by simmering about 30 minutes with some of the ingredients found in the following recipes, such as herbs, onion, and leeks. Any shrimp shells and fish scraps you may have on hand are also good to improve on bottled clam juice, and chicken bones and other chicken scraps will intensify the flavor of canned chicken broth.

Chicken Broth

8 cups water
1 pound chicken parts, preferably
    backs and thighs, all skin and fat
    removed
1 carrot, scraped
1 bay leaf
1½ teaspoons thyme leaves or
    ¼ teaspoon dried

1 onion, peeled
Salt to taste
Several sprigs parsley
1 leek, well washed
6 peppercorns
1 celery stalk

Combine all the ingredients in a large pot and bring to a boil. Skim off the surface scum and fat, cover, and simmer about 1½ to 2 hours. Strain, pressing with the back of a wooden spoon to extract as much liquid as possible.

Fish Broth

8 cups water
½ pound cleaned squid
½ pound cleaned whiting
6 large clams, scrubbed clean
Several sprigs parsley
1 lemon slice
Salt to taste
6 peppercorns

3 large shallots or 1 onion,
   peeled
1 leek, well washed
1 bay leaf
1 celery stalk
1 carrot, scraped
1½ teaspoons thyme leaves or
   ¼ teaspoon dried

Combine all the ingredients in a large pot, bring to a boil, cover, and simmer 30 minutes. Strain, pressing with the back of a wooden spoon to extract as much liquid as possible.

Vegetable Broth

8 cups water
1 onion, peeled
Salt to taste
6 peppercorns
Several sprigs parsley

1½ teaspoons thyme leaves or
   ¼ teaspoon dried
1 celery stalk
1 large carrot, scraped
1 turnip

Combine all the ingredients in a large pot, bring to a boil, cover, and simmer 30 minutes.

Garlic Sauce

(Ajo Aceite)

Makes about 1 cup

3 tablespoons finely chopped
  elongated, mildly hot green
  peppers

5 cloves garlic, chopped
¾ cup extra-virgin olive oil

In a mortar or miniprocessor, mash as finely as possible the peppers and garlic. Incorporate 1 tablespoon of the oil, then gradually stir in the remaining oil.

Salmorreta Red Pepper Sauce

This sauce is used principally as an accompaniment to the Alicante-style Shrimp Paella (page 22) but also makes a great dip for shrimp or other seafood.

Makes about 1 cup

2 small tomatoes (if the sauce is for
  Shrimp Paella, the tomatoes
  have already been prepared)
3 dried sweet red peppers (*ñoras*; see
  Sources, page 215), or 2 mild New
  Mexico peppers, finely chopped,
  or 1 pimiento, finely chopped, and

2 teaspoons sweet paprika,
  preferably Spanish smoked
2 tablespoons minced parsley
6 cloves garlic, minced
¼ teaspoon kosher or sea salt
6 tablespoons extra-virgin olive oil
1 teaspoon lemon juice

Bring a pot of water to a boil, add the whole tomatoes, and simmer about 20 minutes. Skin and seed. Mash to a paste in a mortar or miniprocessor the peppers, parsley, garlic, and salt. Mash in the tomato, then stir in the oil and lemon juice. Allow to sit at least 30 minutes to soften the peppers. This will keep up to 24 hours in the refrigerator.

Spicy Garlic Sauce

Makes about ¾ cup

¼ cup finely chopped red bell
   pepper
1 teaspoon finely chopped fresh hot
   red or green pepper
½ teaspoon ground cumin
½ teaspoon kosher or sea salt

4 cloves garlic, minced
1½ teaspoons thyme leaves or
   ¼ teaspoon dried
¼ teaspoon dried oregano
4 tablespoons minced parsley
½ cup extra-virgin olive oil

Mash to a paste in a mortar or miniprocessor the sweet and hot peppers, cumin, salt, garlic, thyme, oregano, and 2 tablespoons of the parsley. Stir in the oil and remaining 2 tablespoons parsley. Transfer to a serving bowl. This will keep up to 24 hours in the refrigerator.

Pesto Sauce

Makes about ½ cup

2 cups packed fresh basil leaves
3 tablespoons pine nuts
4 cloves garlic, minced
½ cup minced parsley
2 tablespoons grated cured
   Manchego or Parmesan cheese

1 tablespoon olive oil
½ teaspoon salt
Several twists of freshly ground
   pepper
4 tablespoons clam juice or
   vegetable broth

Place all the ingredients except the clam juice in a food processor. Blend until as finely chopped as possible. With the motor running, gradually add the clam juice. This will keep up to 24 hours in the refrigerator.

Spicy Cilantro and Green Pepper Dip

Makes about 1½ cups

1 teaspoon ground cumin
6 cloves garlic, minced
1 teaspoon salt
½ green pepper, finely
   chopped

¾ cup finely chopped cilantro or
   parsley
¼ teaspoon hot pepper flakes
3 tablespoons wine vinegar
½ cup extra-virgin olive oil

In a mortar or miniprocessor, mash to a paste the cumin, garlic, salt, green pepper, cilantro, and pepper flakes. Stir in the vinegar and oil. This will keep up to 24 hours in the refrigerator.

Alioli

Homemade mayonnaise, the base for a fine alioli, is far superior to even the best bottled brands. It can be made in no time in a food processor, so there is no reason not to make it, and it will taste immeasurably better than commercial products because you make it with your own fine olive oil, fresh lemon juice, and, for alioli, fresh garlic.

If uncooked eggs, traditionally used to make mayonnaise, worry you, you can make alioli with any of the egg substitutes available in your supermarket that contain real egg whites. To make plain mayonnaise, just omit the garlic.

Makes about 1½ cups

4 cloves garlic, mashed to a paste in
a mortar or garlic press

¼ teaspoon salt

1 small egg yolk or 3 tablespoons
egg substitute made with egg
whites

1 teaspoon freshly squeezed lemon
juice

1 cup pure (mild-flavored)
olive oil

1 tablespoon hot water

Place in a food processor the garlic, salt, egg, and lemon juice, and beat until well mixed. With the motor running, drizzle in the oil, stopping once or twice to scrape down the sides with a rubber spatula. When all the oil is emulsified, gradually add the hot water. This will keep up to 24 hours in the refrigerator.

Potato Alioli

(Alioli con Patata)

This alioli, which includes some boiled potato, is typically used with Murcia-style rice (page 50) and "Rice on Its Own" El Pegolí (page 48), but it is also appropriate with any other rice dish that calls for alioli.

Makes about 2 cups

1 small (about ¼ pound) red
potato, boiled and peeled

8 cloves garlic, mashed to a paste in
a mortar or garlic press

½ teaspoon freshly squeezed lemon
juice

½ teaspoon salt

1 egg yolk or 3 tablespoons egg
substitute made with egg
whites

1½ cups pure (mild-flavored)
olive oil

In a food processor, beat together the potato, garlic, lemon juice, and salt. Blend in the egg yolk and then slowly drizzle in the oil. This will keep up to 24 hours in the refrigerator.

Mock Alioli

Makes about ¾ cup

¾ cup best quality commercial
   mayonnaise
4 cloves garlic, mashed to a paste in
   a mortar or garlic press

2 teaspoons freshly squeezed
   lemon juice
2 teaspoons extra-virgin
   olive oil

Combine all the ingredients in a bowl. This will keep up to 24 hours in the refrigerator.

Cilantro Mayonnaise

Makes about 1½ cups

1 cup mayonnaise, preferably
   homemade (see Alioli, page 211)
½ cup minced cilantro or
   parsley
2 teaspoons minced capers

4 cloves garlic, mashed to a paste in
   a garlic press
2 tablespoons freshly squeezed
   lemon juice
3 anchovy fillets, minced

Combine all the ingredients in a bowl. This will keep up to 24 hours in the refrigerator.

Sources for Spanish Products

Few food specialty shops stock an adequate supply of foods and equipment used in Spanish cooking. The following sources not only have a great variety of Spanish products but will fill mail orders.

The Spanish Table
1427 Western Avenue
Seattle, WA 98101
206-682-2827

Just about every quality food and wine imported from Spain, including excellent *piquillo* peppers, aged Manchego cheese, serrano ham, squid ink, dried sweet red peppers (*ñoras*), and smoked paprika, can be found here as well as paella pans and earthenware casseroles in all sizes. Prized Valencian *bomba* and several other kinds of rice from Spain are available. Circular gas rings in several sizes to make paella outdoors are also in stock.

La Española
25020 Doble Avenue
Harbor City, CA 90710
310-539-0455

A wonderful selection of homemade Spanish sausage products, including black *morcillas*, plus paella pans and squid ink, cheese, rice, and many other Spanish foods. I am particularly fond of the cocktail-size chorizos, *chistorra* semi-cured sausage, and dry-cured *Cantimpalos*.

Zingerman's
422 Detroit Street
Ann Arbor, MI 48104
313-769-1625 (for mail order); 313-663-3400 (store)

Only the very best Spanish foods are stocked here, from the finest olive oils and sherry vinegars to exquisite *piquillo* peppers and top-of-the-line Spanish cheeses.

Dean & Deluca
560 Broadway
New York, NY 10012
800-221-7714 (for mail order); 212-431-1691 (store)

Paella rice, excellent olive oils, fine saffron, and paella pans.

Draeger's
1010 University Drive
Menlo Park, CA 94025
415-688-0688

Paella pans, Spanish earthenware casseroles, and many Spanish food products.

La Tienda
www.tienda.com
888-472-1022

On-line source for excellent Mas Portell *piquillo* peppers, olive oils, and black olive pâté. Also Spanish rice, serrano ham, caperberries, honey, *turrón* candy, and coffee.

Index

Albariño white wine, 13
Albufera, La, 7, 8
Alhambra, 98
Alicante, 7, 8, 48, 102, 108
Alicante-style paellas, 22, 26, 108
    Monkfish and Almond Paella,
      Alicante Style, 56–57
alioli
    Anchovy Toast with Alioli, 157
    Potato Alioli, 212
    with seafood paellas, 26, 42, 44, 48,
      50, 52
    with tapas and first courses, 155, 156,
      177
Alioli (recipe), 211–13
Almond Crisps, 189
Almond Crisps with Frozen Yogurt and
    Honey, 189, 192
Almond Milk Custard, 185–86
Almond Pine Nut Cookies, 191–92, 202
almonds
    Almond Crisps, 189
    Almond Crisps with Frozen Yogurt
      and Honey, 192
    Almond Milk Custard, 185–86

Almond Pine Nut Cookies, 191–92
    candied, 198
    Chocolate Flan with Almond-
      Flavored Chocolate Sauce, 188–89
    Crispy Almond Tile Cookies, 190–91
    in meat, poultry, and game paellas,
      76, 80, 104
    Monkfish and Almond Paella,
      Alicante Style, 56–57
    Rabbit Paella with Red Pepper and
      Almonds, 84–85
    Raspberry Almond Crisp Sandwiches,
      190
    Sautéed Asparagus in Almond and
      Cumin Sauce, 166
    Tricolor Paella with Cheese,
      Anchovies, and Almonds, 132–33
amontillados, 153–54
anchovies
    Anchovy Toast with Alioli, 157
    Eggplant, Olive, Anchovy, and Caper
      Paella, 142–43
    in tapas and first courses, 164, 173
    Tricolor Paella with Cheese,
      Anchovies, and Almonds, 132–33

Anchovy Toast with Alioli, 157
Andalucía, 40, 98, 165, 177
Andalusian cooking, 164
appetizers, 9
    phyllo, 159
    see also tapas and first courses
Apple Flan Loaf with Carmelized Sugar
    Syrup, 186–87
apples
    Apple Flan Loaf with Caramelized
      Sugar Syrup, 186–87
    Baked Apples with Raisins in Custard
      Sauce, 203–4
apricot preserves
    in desserts, 193
Aragón, 114
Arborio rice, 11
aromatics, 10–11
arroz
    see rice
Arroz a Banda, 8, 48,
Arroz a la Marinera, 46
Arroz al Horno, 148
arroz bomba, 8
    in seafood paellas, 48

Arroz con Costra, 74
Arroz de Caldero, 50
Arroz Empedrat, 136
Arroz Negro, 42
artichokes
    in Catalan-Style Paella, 104
    Cod, Cauliflower, and Artichoke
        Paella, 62–63
    Rabbit, Spinach, and Artichoke
        Paella, 117
asparagus
    in meat, poultry, and game paellas, 76
    Salmon and Asparagus Paella with
        Capers and Dill, 58–59
    Sautéed Asparagus in Almond and
        Cumin Sauce, 166
    in tapas and first courses, 166, 168

baby lamb, 6
bacon, slab
    in meat, poultry, and game paellas,
        90, 110, 112
Baena, 201
banana sauce
    Vanilla Ice Cream with Hot Banana
        Sauce, 196–97
Bar Cervantes (Madrid), 155, 156
Barcelona, 104
basil
    in tapas and first courses, 172
Basque Country, 59
bass
    in seafood paellas, 50
Bean-Pebbled Paella, 136–37
beans
    Bean-Pebbled Paella, 136–37
    Cod, Beans, and Hot Green Pepper
        Paella, 60–61
    Smoked Salmon and Bean Salad, 164
beef, ground
    in meat, poultry, and game paellas,
        112
beef broth
    in vegetable paellas, 148
beef stew meat
    in meat, poultry, and game paellas,
        110
Beretta Superfino Arborio, 11

bienmesabe, 177
black beans
    in vegetable paellas, 136
Black Rice, 13
Black Squid Paella, 42–43
blue crabs
    in seafood paellas, 38
bluefish
    in seafood paellas, 50
Boix, Reme, 8, 90
Boix, Ximo, 8, 90
bomba rice, 11
brandy
    in mixed meat and seafood paellas,
        126
bric, 159
Briviesca, 106
Brochette of Marinated Monkfish, 177
broths, 10, 205, 207–8
    commercial, 207
    in meat, poultry, and game paellas,
        114
    in mixed meat and seafood paellas,
        124
    Monkfish and Almond Paella,
        Alicante Style, 56
    "Rice on Its Own" El Pegolí, 48
    with salt cod paellas, 59
    Seafood Rice, Murcia Style, 50
    Shrimp Paella with Salmorreta Red
        Pepper Sauce, 22
    see also beef broth; Chicken Broth;
        Fish Broth; Vegetable Broth
Brown Rice, Vegetable, and Pine Nut
    Paella, 138–39
Burgos, 106

Cabbage and Chopped Meat Paella,
    112–13
Cabrales blue cheese
    in tapas and first courses, 163
Cádiz, 40, 159, 164
Canary Island dip (mojo), 171
Canary Islands, 94, 173, 196
canelones, 52
capers
    Eggplant, Olive, Anchovy, and Caper
        Paella, 142–43

    in meat, poultry, and game paellas,
        106
    Salmon and Asparagus Paella with
        Capers and Dill, 58–59
    in tapas and first courses, 173
Caramelized Oranges, 200
caramelized sugar syrup, 186
Casa Roberto (restaurant), 36
Casa Ruperto (tapa bar), 70, 178
casseroles, 9, 10, 84, 148
Castellón de la Plana, 7, 8, 90
Castile, 106
Catalan cooking, 64
Catalan Mar y Montaña Paella,
    126–27
Catalan white wine, 13
Catalan-Style Paella, 104–5
Catalunya, 104, 126, 185
    pasta dishes, 52
cauliflower
    Cod, Cauliflower, and Artichoke
        Paella, 62–63
Cenador del Prado, El (restaurant), 158,
    170, 172
centolla (spider crab), 38
cheese
    Cheese and Leek Pastries, 160
    Cheese Pâté with Walnuts and
        Peppers, 163
    Spanish, 154
    in tapas and first courses, 163
    Tricolor Paella with Cheese,
        Anchovies, and Almonds, 132–33
Cheese and Leek Pastries, 160
Cheese Pâté with Walnuts and Peppers,
    163
Chez Victor (restaurant), 163
chicken
    in Catalan-Style Paella, 104
    Chicken, Peppers, and Eggplant
        "Samfaina" Paella, 78–79
    Chicken Paella, Andalusian Style,
        76–77
    Chicken Pepitoria Paella, 80–81
    Crusted Paella with Pork, Chicken,
        and Sausage, 74–75
    in mixed meat and seafood paellas,
        124, 126

Pork, Sausage, Chicken, and Seafood
    Paella, 122–23
Ruperto's Marinated Chicken Paella,
    70–71
Sweet-and-Sour Chicken Paella with
    Honey-Coated Walnuts, 72–73
Chicken, Peppers, and Eggplant
    "Samfaina" Paella, 78–79
Chicken Broth, 207
    canned, 10
Chicken Paella, Andalusian Style, 76–77
Chicken Pepitoria Paella, 80–81
chickpeas
    Baked Riced with Garlic, Potatoes,
        and Chickpeas, 148–49
    Pork, Chickpea, and Red Pepper
        Paella, 102–3
    Spinach, Chickpea, and Pine Nut
        Paella, 134–35
    Tino's Chickpea Stew Paella, 110–11
chiringuitos, 46
chocolate, 188
Chocolate Flan with Almond-Flavored
    Chocolate Sauce, 188–89
chocolate sauce
    Chocolate Flan with Almond-
        Flavored Chocolate Sauce, 188–89
    Frozen Walnut "Cake" with Candied
        Walnuts and Chocolate Sauce, 199
chorizo, 106, 122
    Chorizo and Olive Paella "Santa
        Clara," 106–7
    Chorizo Pastries, 160
    in vegetable paellas, 148
Chorizo and Olive Paella "Santa Clara,"
    106–7
Chorizo Pastries, 160
cilantro
    in meat, poultry, and game paellas,
        116
    Spicy Cilantro and Green Pepper Dip,
        211
    in tapas and first courses, 173
cilantro dips
    Grilled Shrimp with Cilantro Dips,
        171
    with tapas and first courses, 173
Cilantro Mayonnaise, 171, 173, 213

clam juice, 207
    bottled, 10
    substitute for broth, 22
clams
    Clams in Herbed Garlic Sauce, 175
    cleansing, 10
    Garlicky Clam Paella, 32–33
    in seafood paellas, 24, 28, 52
Clams in Herbed Garlic Sauce, 175
clementines, 135
cockles
    in seafood paellas, 24, 28, 32, 52
    in tapas and first courses, 175
Cod, Beans, and Hot Green Pepper
    Paella, 60–61
Cod, Cauliflower, and Artichoke Paella,
    62–63
Cod Paella, Catalan Style, 64–65
cod, salt, 59
cookies, 183, 202
    Almond Crisps, 189
    Almond Crisps with Frozen Yogurt
        and Honey, 192
    Almond Pine Nut Cookies, 191–92
    Crispy Almond Tile Cookies, 190–91
coquille Saint Jacques, 174
Córdoba (province), 165
Córdoba, Fernando, 164
Córdoba, Gonzalo, 40, 164
Córdoba, José Manuel, 164
coriander, 6
Crabmeat Paella with Peas, 38–39
Crackling Caramelized Pine Nuts with Ice
    Cream Bathed in Honey Sauce, 198
Cream Cheese Ice Cream with
    Raspberry Purée, 197
cream sherries, 183
    in desserts, 202
Crispy Almond Tile Cookies, 190–91,
    202
Crusted Paella with Pork, Chicken, and
    Sausage, 74–75
Culinary Institute of America, 178
cumin, 6
    Grilled Shellfish with Tomato and
        Cumin Purée, 170–71
    in meat, poultry, and game paellas,
        70, 114, 116

Sautéed Asparagus in Almond and
    Cumin Sauce, 166
Shrimp with *Cumin-Scented Zucchini*
    Purée, 172
in tapas and first courses, 177
in vegetable paellas, 134, 136
Cumin-Scented Pork and Watercress
    Paella, 94–95
custard sauce
    Baked Apples with Raisins in Custard
        Sauce, 203–4
custards, 183, 190
    Almond Milk Custard, 185–86
    Gossamer Lemon Custard, 185

Dársena, La (restaurant), 8, 102, 108
Delfín Restaurant, 26
Denia, 48
dessert sauces, 184
desserts, 9, 181–204
dill
    Salmon and Asparagus Paella with
        Capers and Dill, 58–59
dips, 11, 205, 211
    Grilled Shrimp with Cilantro Dips, 171
    salmorreta sauce as, 22, 209
    Spicy Cilantro and Green Pepper Dip,
        211
    with tapas and first courses, 173
    tomato purée, 170
    Zucchini Purée as, 172
dried sweet red peppers, 11
    in meat, poultry, and game paellas,
        108
    in seafood paellas, 22, 26, 44, 50, 56
dry apertif sherries, 183
Duck Paella, Sevilla Style, 88–89

Ebro River valley, 114
egg(s)
    chopped, in gazpacho, 165
    ingredient of *pepitoria*, 80
    Rice with Pork, Potato, and Baked
        Eggs, Galician Style, 100–1
    Rosemary-Scented Shellfish and Egg
        Paella, 24–25
    in seafood paellas, 58
    for topping, 80, 81

egg crust
  in meat, poultry, and game paellas, 74
egg substitutes, 211
eggplant
  Chicken, Peppers, and Eggplant
    "Samfaina" Paella, 78–79
  Eggplant, Olive, Anchovy, and Caper
    Paella, 142–43
  Lamb, Lentil, and Eggplant Paella,
    116
Eggplant, Olive, Anchovy, and Caper
  Paella, 142–43
electric ovens, 11
escalivada, 169

Fallas, Las, 95
Faro, El (restaurant), 40, 159, 164
fideuá, 52
first courses, 11, 151–79
fish, 6, 10
  in mixed meat and seafood paellas
  in seafood paellas, 30, 36, 37, 42, 50,
    52, 54
  Shrimp and Fish Balls, 173
Fish Broth, 208
fish scraps
  in seafood paellas, 46
flan
  Apple Flan Loaf with Caramelized
    Sugar Syrup, 186–87
  Chocolate Flan with Almond-
    Flavored Chocolate Sauce, 188–89
flavor enhancers, 10
  rosemary, 24
Fombellida, María Jesús, 186
Fresh Tuna and Rabbit Paella, 124–25
Frozen Walnut "Cake" with Candied
    Walnuts and Chocolate Sauce,
    199
frozen yogurt
  Almond Crisps with Frozen Yogurt
    and Honey, 192
fruit, 104
  with desserts, 183, 186, 202
fruit desserts, 183, 190, 200–4

Galicia, 13, 100
gambas al ajillo, 155

game paellas, 67–117
  wines with, 13
Gandía, 117
garlic, 6, 10
  in alioli, 211
  Baked Riced with Garlic, Potatoes,
    and Chickpeas, 148–49
  Baked Vegetable Medley with Toasted
    Garlic, 168
  Garlic Mushroom Toast, 156
  Garlic Shrimp Toast, 155
  in mash, 126
  in meat, poultry, and game paellas,
    76, 84, 90, 106
  in seafood paellas, 32, 46, 50, 56
  in tapas and first courses, 167, 168,
    173, 174, 175, 177
Garlic Mushroom Toast, 156
Garlic Sauce (ajo aceite), 60, 209
  Clams in Herbed Garlic Sauce, 175
  with seafood paellas, 60
  Tuna Sushi with Roasted Vegetables
    and Garlic Sauce, 169
  see also Spicy Garlic Sauce
Garlic Shrimp Toast, 155
Garlicky Clam Paella, 32–33
garnishes, 5, 12
  hard-boiled eggs, 24
  with meat, poultry, and game
    paellas, 78
  shrimp, 20
gas barbecue/ring grill, 12
gazpacho, 6, 153
  Gazpacho, Córdoba Style, 165
Gazpacho, Córdoba Style, 165
goat cheese
  in tapas and first courses, 163
Golden Rice with Shrimp and Fresh
  Tuna, 26–27
Gossamer Lemon Custard, 185
Granada, 98, 166
grapes
  Marinated Mini Pork Skewers with
    Grapes "Casa Ruperto," 178
  in meat, poultry, and game
    paellas, 90
Green and Yellow Squash Paella with
  Pesto, 28, 146–47

green beans
  in meat, poultry, and game paellas, 76
  in tapas and first courses, 168
green olives
  in meat, poultry, and game
    paellas, 88
green pepper
  Cod, Beans, and Hot Green Pepper
    Paella, 60–61
  Spicy Cilantro and Green Pepper Dip,
    211
green sauce, Spanish, 175
grenadine syrup, 98
Grilled Shellfish with Tomato and
  Cumin Purée, 170–71
Grilled Shrimp with Cilantro Dips,
  171
grouper
  in mixed meat and seafood paellas,
    122
  in seafood paellas, 30, 42, 46, 52,
    54, 56
Guinness Book of World Records, 8
Guriá (restaurant), 59

ham
  in gazpacho, 165
  in meat, poultry, and game paellas,
    106, 112
  in tapas and first courses, 154, 156,
    168, 173, 174
  in vegetable paellas, 136, 144
  see also serrano ham; jamón ibérico
Hemingway, Ernest, 8
herbs, 10
  in broths, 207
  Clams in Herbed Garlic Sauce, 175
  in meat, poultry, and game paellas,
    90, 114
  in mixed meat and seafood paellas,
    124
  in tapas and first courses, 177
Herranz, Tomás, 170, 172
honey, 104
  Almond Crisps with Frozen Yogurt
    and Honey, 192
  Oranges in Honey and Olive Oil
    "Núñez de Prado," 201

honey sauce
  Crackling Caramelized Pine Nuts
    with Ice Cream Bathed in Honey
    Sauce, 198
horchata, 113
hot green peppers
  Cod, Beans, and Hot Green Pepper
    Paella, 60–61
hot red pepper
  in tapas and first courses, 155

ice creams, 183, 190
  Crackling Caramelized Pine Nuts
    with Ice Cream Bathed in Honey
    Sauce, 198
  Cream Cheese Ice Cream with
    Raspberry Purée, 197
  Frozen Walnut "Cake" with Candied
    Walnuts and Chocolate Sauce, 199
  Vanilla Ice Cream with Hot Banana
    Sauce, 196–97
ingredients, 6, 9, 10–11
  preparation, 10
Italy, 52

James, Saint, tomb of, 174
jamón ibérico, 154
jamón serrano, 154
Juanita, 8
Juanjo (chef), 36
Júcar (river), 7

kiwi
  Strawberry or Kiwi Purée, 184
  White Sangria Sorbet with Melon and
    Kiwi, 195

lamb, baby, 6
  Lamb, Lentil, and Eggplant Paella, 116
  Lamb and Red Pepper Paella, 114–15
Lamb, Lentil, and Eggplant Paella, 116
Lamb and Red Pepper Paella, 114–15
lamb paellas
  wines with, 13
leeks
  in broths, 207
  Cheese and Leek Pastries, 160
leftovers, 12

lemon
  Gossamer Lemon Custard, 185
lemon juice
  in mayonnaise, 211
lentils
  Lamb, Lentil, and Eggplant Paella,
    116
Levante, El, 7
lima beans
  in tapas and first courses, 168
littleneck clams
  in seafood paellas, 24, 28, 32, 52
  in tapas and first courses, 175
Llibre del Cuiner, 74
lobster
  Lobster Paella "Casa Roberto," 36–37
  in mixed meat and seafood paellas,
    122
Lobster Paella "Casa Roberto," 36–37
long-grain converted rice, 6

Madrid, 158, 170, 172, 191
  seafood, 161
Manila clams
  in seafood paellas, 24, 28, 32, 52
  in tapas and first courses, 175
marinade
  for Marinated Pork Chop Paella, 96
  Ruperto's Marinated Chicken
    Paella, 70
  in tapas and first courses, 176, 177,
    178
Marinated Mini Pork Skewers with
  Grapes "Casa Ruperto," 178–79
Marinated Pork Chop Paella, 96–97
mash
  see *picada*
mayonnaise
  Cilantro Mayonnaise, 213
  homemade, 211
meat, 6, 10
meat paellas, 67–117, 153
  wines with, 13
  see also mixed meat and seafood
    paellas
meatballs
  Mushroom and Meatball Paella, La
    Dársena Style, 108–9

Mediterranean, 7
Mediterranean diet, 6
melon
  White Sangria Sorbet with Melon and
    Kiwi, 195
Melon Balls in Sweet Sherry, 202
mesclun lettuce
  with tapas and first courses, 164, 178
milk
  Almond Milk Custard, 185–86
mixed meat and seafood paellas, 82,
    119–27
  squid in, 44
Mixed Seafood Paella, 46–47
Mock Alioli, 213
  with seafood paellas, 26, 42, 44, 49,
    50, 52
  with tapas and first courses, 155, 156,
    157
monkfish
  Brochette of Marinated Monkfish,
    177
  in mixed meat and seafood paellas,
    122
  Monkfish, Swiss Chard, and Sesame
    Seed Paella, 54–55
  Monkfish and Almond Paella,
    Alicante Style, 56–57
  in seafood paellas, 30, 36, 42, 46,
    50, 52
  as substitute for salt cod, 60
  in tapas and first courses, 173
Monkfish and Almond Paella, Alicante
  Style, 56–57
Monkfish, Swiss Chard, and Sesame
  Seed Paella, 54–55
Moors, 6, 7, 98, 116, 166, 183, 198
mortar, 10
Murcia, 7, 50
Mushroom and Meatball Paella, La
  Dársena Style, 108–9
mushrooms
  Garlic Mushroom Toast, 156
  in meat, poultry, and game paellas, 76
  in mixed meat and seafood paellas,
    126
  Mushroom and Meatball Paella, La
    Dársena Style, 108–9

mushrooms (*cont'd*)
   Potpourri of Mushrooms Paella,
      144–45
   Quail and Mushroom Paella, 92–93
   Sautéed Mushrooms with Serrano
      Ham and Shrimp, 167
   Scallop and Mushroom Paella, 18–19
mussel broth
   in seafood paellas, 46
Mussel Paella, 34–35
mussels
   cleansing, 10
   in mixed meat and seafood paellas, 122
   Mussel Paella, 34–35
   Mussels Vinaigrette, 176
   in seafood paellas, 24, 52
Mussels Vinaigrette, 176

Navarra, 162
Nola, Ruperto de, 74
ñoras (dried sweet red peppers)
   see dried sweet red peppers
Núñez de Prado brothers, 201
nutmeg, 6
   in meat, poultry, and game paellas,
      70, 80
nuts, 10, 104
   candied, 198, 199
   in mash, 126

olive oils, 6, 9, 10, 11, 21, 165
   in baking, 193
   in mayonnaise, 211
   Oranges in Honey and Olive Oil
      "Núñez de Prado," 201
   in tapas and first courses, 156, 159,
      167, 168, 169
olives
   Chorizo and Olive Paella "Santa
      Clara," 106–7
   Eggplant, Olive, Anchovy, and Caper
      Paella, 142–43
olorosos, 183
onions, 10
   in broths, 207
   in meat, poultry, and game paellas, 78
   in seafood paellas, 32, 58
   in tapas and first courses, 169, 174

oranges
   Caramelized Oranges, 200
   in meat, poultry, and game paellas, 72
   Oranges in Honey and Olive Oil
      "Núñez de Prado," 201
Oranges in Honey and Olive Oil "Núñez
   de Prado," 201
orujo (liqueur), 196
outdoor grill(s), 82
outdoor paella, 8, 12
oven
   cooking paella in, 110
   finishing paella in, 11, 80
oyster mushrooms
   in Chicken Paella, Andalusian Style, 76
   in Garlic Mushroom Toast, 156
   in Green and Yellow Squash Paella
      with Pesto, 146
   in Mushroom and Meatball Paella, La
      Dársena Style, 108
   in Pesto Shellfish Paella, 28
   in Potpourrí of Mushroom Paella, 144
   in Sauteéd Mushrooms with Serrano
      Ham and Shrimp, 167
   in Scallop and Mushroom Paella, 18

paella, 5–6
   a la Valenciana, 82
   de Verduras, 140
   in Valencia, 7–9
   misconceptions about, 9
   Mixta, 122
   pairing Spanish wines with, 13
   serving, 12
   tips for perfect, 10–12
   tricks with, 12
paella maestros, 8
paella pan, 5, 9, 52
   care of, 10
País Valencià (Valencian Country), 7
Palace Hotel (Madrid), 155
Panier Fleuri (restaurant), 186
paprika, 10
   in meat, poultry, and game paellas,
      106, 108
   in mixed meat and seafood paellas,
      124
   in seafood paellas, 44, 56

parsley, 10
   in *picada* (mash), 126
   in meat, poultry, and game paellas, 80
   minced, for garnish, 12
   in seafood paellas, 32, 46
   in tapas and first courses, 175
pasta
   Seafood Pasta Paella, 52–53
pastries
   Cheese and Leek Pastries, 160
   Chorizo Pastries, 160
   Shrimp and Spinach Pastries, 159
pâté
   Cheese Pâté with Walnuts and
      Pepper, 163
Peach Yogurt Torte, 193
Pears Steeped in Red Wine and Sherry
   Syrup, 202–3
peas
   Crabmeat Paella with Peas, 38–39
Pegolí, El (restaurant), 8, 48
Pepica, La (restaurant), 8
pepitoria, 80
peppers, 6, 131
   Cheese Pâté with Walnuts and
      Peppers, 163
   Chicken, Peppers, and Eggplant
      "Samfaina" Paella, 78–79
   in meat, poultry, and game paellas, 76
   Piquillo Pepper Salad with Raisins
      and Pine Nuts, 162
   in tapas and first courses, 155, 169
   tricolor (green, red, and yellow), in
      vegetable paellas, 132
   see also dried sweet red peppers; green
      pepper; red peppers
Pesquera (wine), 13
pesto
   Green and Yellow Squash Paella with
      Pesto, 146–47
   Pesto Shellfish Paella, 28–29
Pesto Sauce, 28, 210
Pesto Shellfish Paella, 28–29
phyllo appetizers, 159
picada
   almonds, garlic, and parsley, 80
   Catalan, 126
   garlic and herbs, 90

Piera, Pepe, 48
pimiento strips
    for garnish, 12
pimientos
    in tapas and first courses, 162
Pincho Moruno, 178
pine nuts
    Almond Pine Nut Cookies, 191–92
    in cod paella, 64
    Crackling Caramelized Pine Nuts
        with Ice Cream Bathed in Honey
        Sauce, 198
    Brown Rice, Vegetable, and Pine Nut
        Paella, 138–39
    in meat, poultry, and game paellas,
        104, 108
    Piquillo Pepper Salad with Raisins
        and Pine Nuts, 162
    Spinach, Chickpea, and Pine Nut
        Paella, 134–35
    in tapas and first courses, 173
Piquillo Pepper Salad with Raisins and
    Pine Nuts, 162
pomegranates
    Pork and Pomegranate Paella, 98–99
pork, 69
    in Catalan-Style Paella, 104
    Crusted Paella with Pork, Chicken,
        and Sausage, 74–75
    Cumin-Scented Pork and Watercress
        Paella, 94–95
    Marinated Mini Pork Skewers with
        Grapes "Casa Ruperto," 178
    Marinated Pork Chop Paella, 96–97
    in meat, poultry, and game paellas,
        108, 110
    Pork, Chickpea, and Red Pepper
        Paella, 102–3
    Pork, Sausage, Chicken, and Seafood
        Paella, 122–23
    Pork and Pomegranate Paella, 98–99
    Rice with Pork, Potato, and Baked
        Eggs, Galician Style, 100–1
Pork, Chickpea, and Red Pepper Paella,
    102–3
Pork, Sausage, Chicken, and Seafood
    Paella, 122–23
Pork and Pomegranate Paella, 98–99

pork paellas
    wines with, 13
portobellos, 144
Potato Alioli, 212
    with seafood paellas, 49, 50
potatoes
    Baked Rice with Garlic, Potatoes, and
        Chickpeas, 148–49
    Rice with Pork, Potato, and Baked
        Eggs, Galician Style, 100–1
    in seafood paellas, 50
Potpourri of Mushrooms Paella, 144–45
poultry paellas, 67–117, 153
    wines with, 13
preparation in advance, 9, 11
    desserts, 185, 200, 202, 203
    seafood paellas, 22, 60, 64
    tapas and first courses, 153, 161, 165,
        176, 177
prosciutto, 154
    in meat, poultry, and game paellas,
        76, 78, 80, 102, 104, 106, 112
    in tapas and first courses, 156, 165,
        167, 168, 173, 174
    in vegetable paellas, 136, 144
purée
    Grilled Shellfish with Tomato and
        Cumin Purée, 170–71
    Raspberry Purée, 184, 197, 200
    Shrimp with Cumin-Scented Zucchini
        Purée, 172
    Strawberry or Kiwi Purée, 184, 185
    tomato, 170
    zucchini, 172

Quail and Mushroom Paella, 92–93

rabbit, 80
    Fresh Tuna and Rabbit Paella, 124–25
    in mixed meat and seafood paellas,
        122
    Rabbit, Spinach, and Artichoke Paella,
        117
    Stewed Rabbit Paella, 86–87
Rabbit, Spinach, and Artichoke Paella,
    117
Rabbit Paella with Red Pepper and
    Almonds, 84–85

rabbit paellas, 83
    wines with, 13
Racó d'Olla (restaurant), 8
raisins
    Baked Apples with Raisins in Custard
        Sauce, 203–4
    in cod paella, 64
    in meat, poultry, and game paellas, 90
    Piquillo Pepper Salad with Raisins
        and Pine Nuts, 162
raspberries
    Cream Cheese Ice Cream with
        Raspberry Purée, 197
    Raspberry Almond Crisp Sandwiches,
        189, 190
Raspberry Almond Crisp Sandwiches,
    189, 190
Raspberry Purée, 184, 197, 100
recipes
    halving/doubling, 10
red peppers
    Lamb and Red Pepper Paella, 114–15
    Pork, Chickpea, and Red Pepper
        Paella, 102–3
    Rabbit Paella with Red Pepper and
        Almonds, 84–85
    see also dried sweet red peppers
red wine
    Pears Steeped in Red Wine and Sherry
        Syrup, 202–3
    Red Wine Sangria Sorbet, 194
Red Wine Sangria Sorbet, 194
Region of the Rices, 6
Ribera del Duero (wine), 13
rice (*arroz*), 5, 6, 7, 9, 17
    Baked Rice with Garlic, Potatoes, and
        Chickpeas, 148–49
    Murcia-style, 212
    "Rice on Its Own" El Pegolí, 48–49
    Seafood Rice, Murcia Style, 50–51
    Soupy Rice with Shellfish, 30–31
    stirring to coat, 11
    Valencia, 7, 8
rice dishes, 9, 110
rice fields, 7
"Rice on Its Own" El Pegolí, 48–49, 212
Rice with Pork, Potato, and Baked Eggs,
    Galician Style, 100–1

Rioja red wine, 13
Riojano, El (bakery), 191
risotto, 6
roe
    in seafood paellas, 38
rosemary
    as flavor enhancer, 24
    in Valencia's Traditional Paella, 82
Rosemary-Scented Shellfish and Egg
        Paella, 24–25
rossejat de fideus, 52
Rueda, 13
Ruperto's Marinated Chicken Paella,
        70–71

saffron, 7, 11, 121
    in meat, poultry, and game paellas,
        114
    in seafood paellas, 30
salad
    Piquillo Pepper Salad with Raisins
        and Pine Nuts, 162
    Smoked Salmon and Bean Salad, 164
    Tuna and Watercress Salad "La
        Trainera," 161
salad dressing, 161
Salamanca, 164
Salcedo, Tino, 110
salmon
    Salmon and Asparagus Paella with
        Capers and Dill, 58–59
    Salmon and Shrimp Toasts, 158
    Smoked Salmon and Bean Salad, 164
Salmon and Asparagus Paella with
        Capers and Dill, 58–59
Salmon and Shrimp Toasts, 158
Salmorejo, 165
salmorreta sauce, 22–23
Salmorreta Red Pepper Sauce, 171, 209
    Shrimp Paella with Salmorreta Red
        Pepper Sauce, 22–23
salt cod
    Cod, Beans, and Hot Green Pepper
        Paella, 60–61
    Cod, Cauliflower, and Artichoke
        Paella, 62–63
    Cod Paella, Catalan Style, 64–65
salt cod paella, 59

Salvador, Marguerite, 163
Salvador, Victor, 163
San Sebastián, 185, 186
Sangria, 13
    Red Wine Sangria Sorbet, 194
    White Sangria Sorbet with Melon and
        Kiwi, 195
Santa Clara convent, Briviesca, 106
Santiago de Compostela, 18, 174
sauces, 11, 205, 209
    Almond and Cumin sauce, 166
    chocolate, 188, 199
    custard, 204
    dessert, 184
    garlic, 60, 175, 209
    green, 175
    honey, 198
    hot banana, 196–97
    Pesto Sauce, 28, 210
    Salmorreta Red Pepper Sauce, 22–23,
        171, 209
    Spicy Garlic Sauce, 140, 210
    white sauce, 159
    see also alioli
sausage
    Chorizo and Olive Paella "Santa
        Clara," 106–7
    Chorizo Pastries, 160
    Crusted Paella with Pork, Chicken,
        and Sausage, 74–75
    in meat, poultry, and game paellas,
        104, 110
    Pork, Sausage, Chicken, and Seafood
        Paella, 122–23
    in vegetable paellas, 148
Sautéed Asparagus in Almond and
        Cumin Sauce, 166
Sautéed Mushrooms with Serrano Ham
        and Shrimp, 167
scallions
    Squid and Scallion Paella, 44–45
Scallop, Shrimp, and Seaweed Paella,
        20–21
Scallop and Mushroom Paella, 13,
        18–19
scallops
    Scallop, Shrimp, and Seaweed Paella,
        20–21

Scallop and Mushroom Paella,
        18–19
Scallops, Santiago Style, 174
    in seafood paellas, 28, 30
    in tapas and first courses, 170
Scallops, Santiago Style, 174
seafood, 6, 48
    in Catalan-Style Paella, 104
    cleansing, 10
    dips for, 209
    first course, 153
    in Madrid, 161
    Pork, Sausage, Chicken, and Seafood
        Paella, 122–23
seafood paellas, 15–65, 153
    wines with, 13
    see also mixed meat and seafood
        paellas
Seafood Pasta Paella, 52–53
Seafood Rice, Murcia Style, 50–51
seaweed
    Scallop, Shrimp, and Seaweed Paella,
        20–21
serrano ham
    in seafood paellas, 18
    in meat, poultry, and game paellas,
        76, 78, 80, 102, 104, 106, 112
    Sautéed Mushrooms with Serrano
        Ham and Shrimp, 167
    in tapas and first courses, 156, 165,
        167, 168, 173, 174
    in vegetable paellas, 136, 144
sesame oil
    in meat, poultry, and game paellas, 90
sesame seeds
    Monkfish, Swiss Chard, and Sesame
        Seed Paella, 54–55
Sevilla, 70, 88, 178
shark
    in tapas and first courses, 177
shellfish
    Grilled Shellfish with Tomato and
        Cumin Purée, 170–71
    Pesto Shellfish Paella, 28–29
    Rosemary-Scented Shellfish and Egg
        Paella, 24–25
    Soupy Rice with Shellfish, 30–31
sherries, 13, 183

in meat, poultry, and game paellas, 70, 76, 80, 88
Melon Balls in Sweet Sherry, 202
in seafood paellas, 40
with tapas, 153–54
sherry syrup
Pears Steeped in Red Wine and Sherry Syrup, 202–3
short-grain rice, 6, 8, 11
shrimp, 48
Garlic Shrimp Toast, 155
Golden Rice with Shrimp and Fresh Tuna, 26–27
Grilled Shrimp with Cilantro Dips, 171
in mixed meat and seafood paellas, 122, 126
Salmon and Shrimp Toasts, 158
Sautéed Mushrooms with Serrano Ham and Shrimp, 167
Scallop, Shrimp, and Seaweed Paella, 20–21
in seafood paellas, 24, 28, 30, 42
Shrimp and Fish Balls, 173
Shrimp and Spinach Pastries, 159
Shrimp Paella, Alicante-Style, 209
Shrimp Paella with Salmorreta Red Pepper Sauce, 22–23
Shrimp with Cumin-Scented Zucchini Purée, 172
in tapas and first courses, 158, 159, 170
Shrimp and Fish Balls, 173
Shrimp and Spinach Pastries, 159
Shrimp Paella, Alicante-Style, 209
Shrimp Paella with Salmorreta Red Pepper Sauce, 22–23
Shrimp with Cumin-Scented Zucchini Purée, 172
Smoked Salmon and Bean Salad, 164
snails, 82
snap peas/snow peas
in meat, poultry, and game paellas, 106
socarrat, 8, 12
with Valencia's Traditional Paella, 82
sorbets
Red Wine Sangria Sorbet, 194

Strawberry and Wine Vinegar Sorbet, 195–96
White Sangria Sorbet with Melon and Kiwi, 195
Soupy Rice with Shellfish, 30–31
sources for Spanish products, 215–16
Spain
regions of, 6, 7
revolution in cooking in, 8–9
Spanish cheese, 154
Spanish diet, 6
Spanish products
sources for, 215–16
Spanish smoked paprika, 10
Spanish Tetilla, 160
Spanish wines/sherries, 13, 183
Spicy Cilantro and Green Pepper Dip *(mojo),* 211
Spicy Garlic Sauce, 210
Vegetable Paella with Spicy Garlic Sauce, 140–41
see also Garlic Sauce
spinach
Rabbit, Spinach, and Artichoke Paella, 117
sautéed with raisins and pine nuts, 64
Shrimp and Spinach Pastries, 159
Spinach, Chickpea, and Pine Nut Paella, 134–35
Spinach, Chickpea, and Pine Nut Paella, 134–35
squash
Green and Yellow Squash Paella with Pesto, 146–47
squid
Black Squid Paella, 42–3
in mixed meat and seafood paellas, 122
in seafood paellas, 22, 24, 46, 49, 52
Squid and Scallion Paella, 44–45
Stewed Squid Paella "El Faro," 40–41
in tapas and first courses, 170
Squid and Scallion Paella, 44–45
squid ink, 42
Stewed Rabbit Paella, 86–87
Stewed Squid Paella "El Faro," 40–41
stews
Lamb and Red Pepper Paella, 114–15

Stewed Rabbit Paella, 86–87
Stewed Squid Paella "El Faro," 40–41
Tino's Chickpea Stew Paella, 110–11
Strawberry and Wine Vinegar Sorbet, 195–96
Strawberry or Kiwi Purée, 184, 185
substitutes, 9
for Spanish cured ham, 154
for eggs, 199, 211
in meat, poultry, and game paellas, 82, 98
in seafood paellas, 50, 56, 60
suckling pig, 6
surf and turf, 124, 126
sweet sherries, 183
Sweet-and-Sour Chicken Paella with Honey-Coated Walnuts, 72–73
sweet-and-sour flavors, 98
Swiss chard
Monkfish, Swiss Chard, and Sesame Seed Paella, 54–55
in vegetable paellas, 136
swordfish
in tapas and first courses, 177

tapas, 70, 151–79
sherries with, 183
Tasca del Puerto, La (restaurant), 8, 90
Tetilla cheese, 160
thyme
in meat, poultry, and game paellas, 70
in seafood paellas, 46
Tino's Chickpea Stew Paella, 110–11
Tío Pepe (sherry) 153
toast
Anchovy Toast with *Alioli,* 157
Garlic Mushroom Toast, 156
Garlic Shrimp Toast, 155
Salmon and Shrimp Toasts, 158
Tomato and cumin purée, 170–71
tomatoes, 6
Grilled Shellfish with Tomato and Cumin Purée, 170–71
in meat, poultry, and game paellas, 78, 114
in seafood paellas, 22, 56
in tapas and first courses, 169
in vegetable paellas, 148

tommaley
    in seafood paellas, 36, 38
Toñi Vicente (restaurant), 18
toppings, 5
    in meat, poultry, and game
        paellas, 80
    Salmon and Asparagus Paella with
        Capers and Dill, 58
torte
    Peach Yogurt Torte, 193
Trainera, La (restaurant), 161
Tricolor Paella with Cheese, Anchovies,
    and Almonds, 132–33
tropezones, 26
Tropical Paella "Tasca del Puerto,"
    90–91
tuna
    Fresh Tuna and Rabbit Paella, 124–25
    Golden Rice with Shrimp and Fresh
        Tuna, 26–27
    in tapas and first courses, 177
    Tuna and Watercress Salad "La
        Trainera," 161
    Tuna with Roasted Vegetable and
        Garlic Sauce, 169
Tuna and Watercress Salad "La Trainera,"
    161
Tuna with Roasted Vegetables and Garlic
    Sauce, 169
Turia (river), 7
turrón, 145

Urepel (restaurant), 185

Valencia, 6, 7–9, 30, 36, 48, 108, 117
    "baked rice" dishes, 110
    bomba rice from, 11
    fideuá, 52
    mixed paellas in, 122
    oranges, 72
    original paella, 85
Valencia's Traditional Paella, 82–83
Vanilla Ice Cream with Hot Banana
    Sauce, 196–97
Vegetable Broth, 208
    canned, 10
vegetable first course, 153
Vegetable Paella with Spicy Garlic Sauce,
    140–41
vegetable paellas, 64, 129–49
vegetables, 6, 7
    Baked Vegetable Medley with Toasted
        Garlic, 168
    frozen, 10
    in meat, poultry, and game paellas, 76
    Tuna with Roasted Vegetables and
        Garlic Sauce, 169
Vicente, Toñi, 18
Villa Turística de Bubión, 166
vinaigrettes, 6
    with tapas and first courses, 158, 161,
        163, 164
Viveros, Los (restaurant), 36

walnuts
    Cheese Pâté with Walnuts and
        Pepper, 163

Frozen Walnut "Cake" with Candied
        Walnuts and Chocolate Sauce, 199
    in meat, poultry, and game paellas, 90
walnuts, honey-coated
    Sweet-and-Sour Chicken Paella with
        Honey-Coated Walnuts, 72–73
watercress
    Cumin-Scented Pork and Watercress
        Paella, 94–95
    in meat, poultry, and game paellas, 98
    Tuna and Watercress Salad "La
        Trainera," 161
White Sangria Sorbet with Melon and
    Kiwi, 195
white sauce, 159
white wine
    in tapas and first courses, 175
whiting
    in seafood paellas, 49
wine vinegar
    Strawberry and Wine Vinegar Sorbet,
        195–96
wines, 13, 183
wood-burning stove, 8

yogurt
    Almond Crisps wtih Frozen Yogurt
        and Honey, 192
    Peach Yogurt Torte, 193

zucchini
    Shrimp with Cumin-Scented Zucchini
        Purée, 172